Anthony Neilson

The Wonderful World of Dissocia

and

Realism

D1148584

Methuen Drama

Published by Methuen Drama, 2007

1 3 5 7 9 10 8 6 4 2

Methuen Drama
A & C Black Publishers Limited
38 Soho Square
London W1D 3HB
www.acblack.com

ISBN: 978 0 7136 8715 6

A CIP catalogue record for this book
is available from the British Library

Typeset by Country Setting, Kingsdown, Kent
Printed and bound in Great Britain by
Bookmarque Ltd, Croydon, Surrey

The National Theatre of Scotland
presents the Edinburgh International Festival,
Drum Theatre Plymouth and Tron Theatre Glasgow's
production of

The Wonderful World
of Dissocia

by Anthony Neilson

The Wonderful World of Dissocia

Anthony Neilson

CAST

Passenger 3 Oath-taker Attendant; Goat; Biffer; Nurse 2	James Cunningham
Lisa	Christine Entwisle
Passenger 4; Oath-taker; Ticket; Dr Clark	Alan Francis
Passenger 1; Oath-taker Attendant; Jane; Violinist; Dot	Amanda Hadingue
Guard 1; Inhibitions; Vince	Jack James
Passenger 2; Oath-taker Attendant; Britney; Nurse 1	Claire Little
Guard 2; Laughter; Dr Faraday	Matthew Pidgeon
Victor Hesse; Oath-taker Attendant; Argument; Nurse 3	Barnaby Power

Director	Anthony Neilson
Designer	Miriam Buether
Lighting Designer	Chahine Yavroyan
Sound Designer/Composer	Nick Powell
Assistant Designer	Claire Halleran

The Wonderful World of Dissocia
was first performed at the Tron Theatre, Glasgow
and opened at the Royal Lyceum Theatre as part of
the 2004 Edinburgh International Festival.
It was revived by the National Theatre of Scotland
in 2007 and toured the UK as follows:

Tron Theatre, Glasgow	28th February to 10th March
Dundee Rep Theatre	20th to 24th March
Royal Court, London (Jerwood Theatre Downstairs)	28th March to 21st April
Theatre Royal, Plymouth	24th to 28th April
Oxford Playhouse	1st to 5th May
Warwick Arts Centre	8th to 12th May
York Theatre Royal	22nd to 26th May
Traverse Theatre, Edinburgh	6th to 9th June
Northern Stage, Newcastle	12th to 16th June

Thanks
Neil Anderson, Adam Bullock, Alex Bynoth, Pamela Carter,
Fran Craig, Mark Hughes, J&B Scenery, Sergey Jakovsky,
Elaine Johnston, Julie Kirsop, Jennifer Loof,
Sarah McCaughey, Jo Masson, Louise Oliver, Kirsty Paton,
Hazel Price, Malcolm Rogan, Peter Screen, Raymond Short,
Kathryn Smith, Ros Steen, Simon Stokes, Stephanie Thorburn,
Karen Toal, Iain Urquart, Amy Vaughan-Spencer,
Sarah Willson, David Young, and all at
the Theatre Royal Plymouth, Tron Theatre Glasgow
and the Edinburgh International Festival.

THE COMPANY

Anthony Neilson
(Writer & Director)

Anthony Neilson is an Artistic Associate of NTS, for whom he directed *Home: Edinburgh* and wrote and directed *Realism*, in an EIF co-production in 2006. A creator of pioneering, taboo-breaking new work, Anthony Neilson writes and directs witty, bold and compassionate plays that explore unchartered psychological territories.

Previous work includes: *The Lying Kind* (Royal Court), *Stitching* (The Red Room & Bush Theatre – Time Out Off-West End Award), *Edward Gant's Amazing Feats of Loneliness* (Drum Theatre, Plymouth), *The Censor* (The Red Room at The Finborough & Royal Court – The Writers Guild Award 1997 for Best Fringe Play and The Time Out Live Award 1997), *The Night Before Christmas* (The Red Room), *Penetrator* (Traverse Theatre & Royal Court), *The Year Of The Family* (Finborough) and *Normal* (Edinburgh Festival). Films include: *The Debt Collector* and *Deeper Still*. Anthony has also written for radio.

Miriam Buether (Designer)

Miriam's design credits include: *Generations* (Young Vic), *Pool (No Water)* (Frantic Assembly), *Realism* (National Theatre of Scotland & EIF), *Long Time Dead* (Paines Plough & Drum Theatre), *The Bee* (Soho Theatre), *Unprotected* (Liverpool Everyman), *Trade* (RSC), *After the End* (Paines Plough & Bush Theatre), *The Death of Klinghoffer* (Scottish Opera), *Way to Heaven* (Royal Court), *Platform* (ICA), *The Wonderful World of Dissocia* (Tron Theatre, Plymouth Drum Theatre & EIF), for which she won the Critics' Award for Theatre in Scotland, *Guantanamo* (Tricycle Theatre), *The People Next Door* (Traverse Theatre), *The Dumb Waiter* (Oxford Playhouse), *Red Demon* (Young Vic), *Eskimo Sisters* (Southwark Playhouse).

Her dance credits include *Outsight* and *Tender Hooks* (Gulbenkian Foundation Lisbon), *Toot* and *Possibly Six* (Les Grand Ballets Canadiens de Montréal), *Track* (Scottish Dance Theatre), *Body of Poetry* (Komische Oper, Berlin) and *7DS* (Sadler's Wells). Miriam has also designed installations at the KX Kampnagel Gallery and the Kunsthaus, Hamburg, and the National Gallery in Sopot, Poland. She won the 1999 Linbury Prize for Stage Design.

James Cunningham
(Passenger 3; Oath-taker Attendant; Goat; Biffer; Nurse 2)

Theatre work includes: *Petrol Jesus Nightmare #5* (Traverse Theatre), *One Day All This Will Come To Nothing* (Traverse Theatre), *The Wonderful World of Dissocia* (Tron Theatre, Drum Theatre & EIF), *Cleansed* (Royal Court), *Trainspotting* (Citizens', Bush Theatre & Traverse Theatre), *Green Field*

(Traverse Theatre), *Passing Places* (Derby Playhouse & Greenwich Theatre), *Abandonment* (Traverse Theatre), *You'll Have Had Your Hole* (London Astoria II), *Marabou Stork Nightmares* (Citizens' & Leicester Haymarket), *Penetrator* (Traverse Theatre & Royal Court), *Love of a Good Man* (Old Red Lion & Sherman Theatre, Cardiff).

Television work includes: *Murphy's Law* (Tiger Aspect), *Taggart* (SMG), *Rockface* (BBC) *Bumping The Odds* (Wall To Wall TV), *Rebus* (ITV), *Pie In The Sky* (SelecTV), *Writers And Nation, A Mug's Game, The Garden* (BBC Scotland), *Roughnecks II* (First Choice). Film work includes: *Sixteen Years of Alcohol* (Tartan Works Ltd), *War Requiem,* (BBC Film), *Snatch* (Ska Films).

Christine Entwistle (Lisa)

Theatre work includes: *The Wonderful World of Dissocia* (Tron Theatre, Drum Theatre & EIF), for which she won a Herald Angel and C.A.T.S. Best Actress Award, *The Wedding* (Scarlet Theatre & Southwark Playhouse), *Edward Gant's Amazing Feats of Loneliness* (Theatre Royal, Plymouth), *I Am Dandy and Vanity Play* (South Bank), *Breathtaking, Bok and Vincenzi, People Shows: 100, 101 and 103 & Vassa* (Almeida at the Albery), *And A Family Affair,* (Theatre Clwyd), *C'est Vauxhall!* (The Duckie Company). Television and film work includes: *At*

Dawning (Winner of 2002 Year's Golden Bear Award), *Deeper Still* (Channel 4 Films), *Storm Damage, Holby City, Attachments, Dalziel and Pascoe* (BBC), *Where The Heart Is* (ITV).

Christine also works as a solo artist, writer and director and is half of the cabaret double act *Wonderhorse,* whose new show *The Olden Days* will premiere later this year at the London Music Hall Society.

Alan Francis (Passenger 4; Oath-taker; Ticket; Dr Clark)

Theatre work includes: *Francis & Power – Deep Dark Cuts, Jeffrey Dahmer Is Unwell* (Paula van Hagen), *The Wonderful World of Dissocia* (Tron Theatre, Drum Theatre & EIF), *Take A Chance On Me* (New End, Hampstead), *Penetrator (*Traverse Theatre & Royal Court), *Clobbered, Miss Conceptions* (RBM), *The Electronic Dark Age* (Edinburgh Fringe). Television work includes: *Pulling, Last Laugh, Spy, Alistair McGowan's Big Impression, The 11 O'Clock Show, Stand Up, Comedy Nation, Between The Lines, Knowing Me, Knowing Yule, Various, Alas Smith and Jones, Fist Of Fun, Alexi Sayle Show, Lenny Goes To Town* (BBC). Radio work includes: *It's That Jo Caulfield Again, Three Off The Tee, Stamp Collecting With Legs, The Alan Davies Show* (BBC Radio 4), *Colin,* nominated for Song Award (BBC Radio 5). Film work includes: *The Debt Collector* (Channel 4 Films).

Amanda Hadingue
(Passenger 1; Oath-taker
Attendant; Jane; Violinist; Dot)

Theatre work includes: *Of All
The People In All The World*
(Stan's Cafe Theatre Company),
The Birthday Show (People
Show), *Vanity Play* (David Gale
Company), *The Obituary Show*
(Bush Theatre & People Show),
*The Wonderful World of
Dissocia* (Tron Theatre, Drum
Theatre & EIF), *Live From
Paradise* (Station House Opera),
The Railway Children (West
End Peacock Theatre &
Nottingham Playhouse), *Good
and True, Be Proud Of Me*
(Stan's Cafe), *The Emperor and
the Nightingale* (Watermill
Theatre), *The Silver Sword*
(Nottingham Playhouse*), How
To Behave* (Hampstead Theatre
& Station House Opera), *Great
Expectations* (Unicorn Theatre*),
Storm* (Contact Theatre), *I Am
Dandy* (David Gale Company),
Cure (IOU Theatre), *Digging For
Ladies* (Amy Roadstone
Productions), *Country Dance*
(Graeme Miller Company),
Princess Sharon (Scarlet
Theatre), *Ocean of Storms*
(Stan's Cafe), *The Fruit Has
Turned To Jam In The Fields*
(Scarlet Theatre), *Clair De Luz,
A Cursed Place* (Insomniac
Productions).

Television work includes: *Lead
Balloon* (Open Mike
Productions), *Serves You Right*
(Granada Television), *The
Weatherhouse* (BBC2). Film
work includes: *The Queen*
(Granada Screen). Radio work
includes: *Fly By Night, Fresh
Figs At 5 a.m.* (BBC Radio 4).

Claire Halleran
(Assistant Designer)

Claire Halleran is a graduate of
Glasgow School of Art and has a
Master's in Fine Art from Queen
Margaret University College.
Claire has designed shows for a
range of companies including:
Giant Productions (*The Puzzle*)
Birds of Paradise (*Mouth of
Silence*; *Brazil 12, Scotland 0*)
Fish & Game (*Otter Pie*),
Playgroup (*The Art Of
Swimming*), National Theatre
of Scotland Young Company
(*Oedipus The King*), Cat in a
Cup (*The Vinegar Doll*; *I Love
You Numb*; *Such is Nature*) and
numerous shows with the
Lyceum Youth Theatre. Claire
has also worked with Suspect
Culture (*Lament*; *One, Two…*;
8000m) Stellar Quines,
benchtours, Theatre Workshop,
Grid Iron and The Edinburgh
International Science Festival.

Jack James
(Guard 1; Inhibitions; Vince)

Theatre work includes: *The
Menu* (National Theatre),
Richard II (Old Vic), *The
Wonderful World of Dissocia*
(Tron Theatre, Drum Theatre &
EIF). *The Coast of Utopia, The
Merchant of Venice,
Summerfolk, Money, Troilus
and Cressida,* (National
Theatre), *Macbeth, King John,
Much Ado About Nothing, The
Plantagenets, Love's Labours
Lost, Kissing the Pope* (RSC),
*Satellite City by Boyd Clack,
Song from A Forgotten City by
Ed Thomas, Heaven, The Plot,
The Origin of Table Manners,*

The Burning of the Dancers, Honey to Ashes, Bar Valentino, The Conspiracy of Silk, Listing, You Do It (Devised). Film work includes: *The Merchant of Venice, Hedd Wynn.*

Claire Little
(Passenger 2; Oath-taker Attendant; Britney; Nurse 1)

Claire trained at LAMDA. Her theatre work includes: *A Midsummer Night's Dream* (Stafford Castle), *Slender* (Mapping 4D), *A Midsummer Night's Dream* (Natural Perspectives), *Live From Paradise* (Station House Opera), *The Wonderful World of Dissocia* (Tron Theatre, Drum Theatre & EIF), *Six Degrees of Separation* (Manchester Royal Exchange), *Vertigo* (Mapping 4D), *Shakespeare in Art* (Dulwich Picture Gallery), *Theseus and The Minotaur* (Moveable Feast). Film work includes: *Really* (Day for Night Films), *Vagabond Shoes* (Ugly Duckling Films), *Human Resources* (Elbow Grease Productions).

Matthew Pidgeon
(Guard 2; Laughter; Dr Faraday)

Born in the U.S., Matthew trained at the RSAMD. His theatre credits include: *The Wonderful World of Dissocia* (Tron Theatre, Drum Theatre & EIF), *The Lying Kind* (Royal Court), *Edward Gant's Amazing Feats of Loneliness* (Drum Theatre), *The Nest* (Traverse Theatre), *8,000m* (Suspect Culture), *Realism* (National Theatre of Scotland & EIF), *The Tempest* (Tron Theatre), *Pinocchio* (Lyceum). TV credits include: *Casualty, Lee and Herring* (BBC), *Taggart* (ITV*), Holby City* (BBC). Film credits include: *The Winslow Boy, State and Main, A Shot at Glory, Chopsticks.* Radio credits include: *McLevy, Kaffir Lillies, The Holly and the Ivy, Devastated Areas, Greenmantle.*

Nick Powell
(Composer & Sound Designer)

Nick Powell's theatre composing credits include *Realism* (National Theatre of Scotland & EIF) and *Wolves in the Walls* (National Theatre of Scotland & Improbable). As a founding member of Glasgow's Suspect Culture, he has developed and scored twelve of their shows, including *Timeless, Mainstream, Casanova, Lament, One Two...* and *8000m*. His other theatre credits include *Lifegame* and *Animo* (Improbable), *Pyrenees, Mercury Fur, The Drowned World* and *Splendour* (Paines Plough), *Tiny Dynamite* (Frantic Assembly), *Playhouse Creatures*, and *Mr Heracles* (West Yorkshire Playhouse).

He composed the score for last year's award-winning *Hamelin* (Madrid's Animalario) and has composed soundtracks for Channel 4 (including the BAFTA-winning *Beneath the Veil*), ITV, BBC Television and CBS. He co-wrote the orchestral score for PBS's *Luther* and wrote the soundtrack for HBO's

Death in Gaza. As one half of the duo OSKAR, he has performed in Milan for Prada fashion shows, exhibited at the Victoria and Albert Museum and recorded for Universal Digital. His current projects include co-writing a music-theatre piece supported by the National Theatre Studio and scoring *Marat Sade* for the Spanish National Theatre.

Barnaby Power
(Victor Hesse; Oath-taker Attendant; Argument; Nurse 3)

Theatre work includes: *Faust*, Parts 1 & 2 (Royal Lyceum), *Laurel and Hardy* (Royal Lyceum), *The Wonderful World of Dissocia* (Tron Theatre, Drum Theatre & EIF), *Edward Gant's Amazing Feats of Loneliness* (Plymouth Theatre Royal), *The Order of Memories* (BAC), *I Am Dandy* (David Gale Company), *Deep Dark Cuts* (RBM), *Sofa* (National Theatre of Romania), *The Suicide Club* (Hen & Chickens), *The Lost Island* (Deadface Theatre Co.), *Pangandaran* (Old Red Lion & Camden People's Theatre), *I Wanna Be Wolfman, Exhibit* (Bodies in Flight). Radio work includes: *Stamp-Collecting with Legs* (BBC Radio 4), *Be Prepared* (BBC Radio 4).

Chahine Yavroyan
(Lighting Designer)

Chahine has designed the lighting for theatre, opera, dance, objects, clothes, buildings, site-specific projects, interiors and exteriors. His theatre credits include *Elizabeth Gordon Quinn* (National Theatre of Scotland), *The Death of Klinghoffer* (Scottish Opera & EIF), *Realism* (National Theatre of Scotland & EIF), *The Cosmonaut's Last Message* (Tron Theatre), *San Diego* (Tron Theatre & EIF), *Outlying Islands, 15", Iron, The Speculator, Gagarin Way, Anna Weiss, King of the Fields, Knives in Hens, Perfect Days* and *The Architect* (Traverse Theatre), *Gilt* (7:84) and *Dumbstruck* (Dundee Rep). Chahine has also worked at the Royal Court, the Royal Exchange, Manchester, Hampstead Theatre, Nottingham Playhouse, The Crucible Theatre, Sheffield, the Bush Theatre, the Young Vic and the King's Head, as well as Paines Plough, Rose English, Lindsay Kemp, and countless People Shows.

Chahine's dance credits include productions with Jasmin Vardimon, Yolande Snaith Theatredance, Rosemary Lee, Bock and Vincenzi, Walkerdance, Ricochet and Anatomy Dance. He has also worked for the ENO at the London Coliseum. His site-specific projects include *Salisbury Proverbs* for Station House Opera, *Dreamwork* at St Pancras Chambers, *Spa* at the Elizabeth Garrett Anderson Hospital, *Deep End* at Marshall St. Baths, the City of Bologna's New Year's Eve celebrations and the Coin Street Museum. Chahine has also lit fashion shows for Givenchy, Clemens-Ribeiro, Chalayan and Ghost.

EDINBURGH
INTERNATIONAL
FESTIVAL

Realism Anthony Neilson

CAST

Paul; Galloway; Independent Politician; Minstrel; Bystander	Paul Blair
Angie; Presenter; Bystander	Louise Ludgate
Laura; Right-wing Politician	Shauna Macdonald
Stuart McQuarrie	Stuart McQuarrie
Father; Pundit; Simon; Minstrel	Sandy Neilson
Mother; Left-wing Politician	Jan Pearson
Mullet; Minstrel	Matthew Pidgeon

Director	Anthony Neilson
Designer	Miriam Buether
Lighting Designer	Chahine Yavroyan
Sound Designer/Composer	Nick Powell
Assistant Director	Gemma Fairley

Realism
was first performed on the 14th August 2006
at the Royal Lyceum Theatre
as part of the Edinburgh International Festival.

THE COMPANY

Paul Blair
(Paul; Galloway; Independent
Politician; Minstrel; Bystander)

Theatre work includes: *The
Escapologist* (Suspect Culture);
East Coast Chicken Supper
(Traverse Theatre) *Anna
Karenina* (Royal Lyceum);
Shining Souls (Tron Theatre &
V.amp); and *Flight* at the
National Theatre. He is an
associate member of the
Dundee Rep Ensemble, where
his roles include Macbeth.
Television credits include: *Sea
of Souls, Takin' over the
Asylum, The Lee and Herring
Show, Ruffian Hearts* and
Bumpin' the Odds (BBC); *The
Ruth Rendell Mysteries* (ITV);
and *Taggart* (STV). His films
include: *This Year's Love,
Hallam Foe, Legend of the
Loch* and *Heavenly Pursuits*. As
co-founder of the production
company Brocken Spectre, he
has produced two short films:
The Turning Tide and *Rank*,
which was nominated for a
BAFTA for Best Short Film.

Gemma Fairlie
(Assistant Director)

Gemma's directing credits
include: Moira Buffini's *Silence*
(The Other Place and Arcola);
For Every Passion Something
(RSC Learning Residency in
USA); Mike Poulton's *St
Erkenwald* (Oxford School
of Drama); *Protect Me From
What I Want*, a devised piece
(Young Vic Studio); Shelagh
Stephenson's *Memory of
Water* (Baron's Court); and
David Mamet's *The Frog Prince*
and Franca Rame's *Same Old
Story* (Cockpit Theatre). She
was Assistant Director on the
RSC's tour of *Julius Caesar* and
The Two Gentlemen of Verona,
a national tour of *Carousel* and
Happy Yet? (The Gate). In 2006
she attended the National
Theatre Directors' Course and
has recently received a Young
Directors' Bursary from the
Gate Theatre.

Louise Ludgate
(Angie; Presenter; Bystander)

Louise Ludgate was born in
Aberdeen and trained at the
RSAMD. Her recent theatre
work includes: *Home: Glasgow*
(National Theatre of Scotland);
Trojan Women (Theatre
Cryptic); *Jeff Koons* (Actors
Training Company); *When the
Dons Were Kings* (Lemon
Tree); *Iron* (Traverse Theatre &
Royal Court); *Lament,
Mainstream* and *Casanova*
(Suspect Culture); *Greta*
(Traverse Theatre); *The Devils*
and *The Crucible* (The Arches).
Her television credits include:
Spooks, Sea of Souls, The Key
and *Tinsel Town* (BBC); *High
Times* and *Taggart* (SMG). Her
films include: *Kissing, Tickling
and Being Bored, No Man's
Land* and *Goodbye Happy
Ending*. Her radio credits
include: *Due South* and *Mrs
McCauly Is Carried Forward*
(BBC Radio 4) *Outlying Islands,
The Commuter* (BBC Radio 3).

Shauna Macdonald
(Laura; Right-wing Politician)

Shauna Macdonald was born in Malaysia and trained at the RSAMD. Her recent theatre work includes *A View from the Bridge* (Dundee Rep & West Yorkshire Playhouse), *Home: Edinburgh* (National Theatre of Scotland), *Victory* (Royal Lyceum), *Pal Joey* (Citizens'), and *The Tempest* (Brunton Theatre). Her recent television work includes: *Sea of Souls*, *Spooks*, *State of Play* and *Murder Rooms* (BBC), *Taggart* (SMG). Recent film appearances include: *Mutant Chronicles*, *Jetsam*, *The Descent*, *Niceland*, *The Rocket Post*, *Late Night Shopping*, *Daybreak* and *The Debt Collector*. Her recent radio work includes *Soft Falls the Sound of Eden* (BBC).

Stuart McQuarrie
(Stuart McQuarrie)

Stuart McQuarrie's recent theatre credits include *The God of Hell* and *The Dark* (Donmar Warehouse); *Scenes from the Big Picture* and *Ivanov* (National Theatre), *The Taming of the Shrew* (RSC), *Our Country's Good* (Out of Joint), *Cleansed* (Royal Court), *Shining Souls* (Tron Theatre & V.amp), and *The Government Inspector* (Almeida). His television appearances include: *The Bill* and *Golden Hour* (Thames Television); *Rebus* (SMG); *A Very Social Secretary* *(More 4); *Ghost Squad* and *Marian Again* (Company

Pictures); *Nathan Barley* (TalkBack Productions); *Life Begins* and *The Deal* (Granada); *The Way We Live Now* and *The Echo* (BBC); and *Four Fathers* (Sally Head Productions). His films include: *Young Adam*, *28 Days Later*, *The Honeytrap*, *The Life of Stuff*, *Trainspotting* and *Love Me Tender* (BBC Scotland).

Sandy Neilson
(Father; Pundit; Simon; Minstrel)

Sandy Neilson was born in Invernesshire and trained at the RSAMD. He was a drama officer for the Scottish Arts Council and Artistic Director of the Fifth Estate Theatre Company and spent three years as an actor and director with the Dundee Repertory Ensemble, with whom he toured throughout Scotland and to Tehran. His theatre credits include: *Tales from Hollywood* (Perth Theatre); *Cyprus* (Mull Theatre); *Macbeth* (Theatre Babel); *Death of a Salesman* (Royal Lyceum); *Ghosts* (Lyric Theatre, Belfast); and *Laird O'Grippy*, *Dancing at Lughnasa*, *The Seagull* and *The Winter's Tale* (Dundee Rep). His television credits include Father Brian in *Secret of the Stars*; *Still Game IV*, *Cathedral*, *End of Story: Ed McBain*, *The Greeks* and *Mr Wymi II* (BBC); and *Taggart*, *Penthouse and Pavement* (SMG). Films include *Retribution*, *Young Adam*, *A Shot at Glory*, *The Debt Collector* and *The Winter Guest*.

Jan Pearson
(Mother; Left-wing Politician)

Jan Pearson's recent theatre work includes *The Norman Conquests* (Theatre Clywd); *Angel Magick* (Serious Music at the Royal Albert Hall); *Princess Sharon* and *The Sisters* (Scarlet Theatre); *The Jinx* (Paines Plough & Bridewell Theatre); *Sabina* (Bush Theatre); *The Censor*, *Tantamount Esperance* and *Heredity* (Royal Court); *Beauty and the Beast* (Young Vic & RSC); and *Grimm Tales* (Haymarket, Leicester). Her television work includes *Silent Witness*, *Doctors* and *Holby City* (BBC); *Where the Heart Is* and *London Bridge* (Granada); *Cops* (World Television); *The Bill* (Thames Television); *Underworld* (Hat Trick Productions); and *Inspector Wycliffe* and *The Chief* (HTV). Her films include: *The Invitation* and *Martha Meet Frank, Daniel and Laurence*. Recent radio work includes: *The Nationalisation of Women* and *Flowers of the Dead Red Sea* (BBC Radio 3), *May and the Snowman* (BBC Radio 4) and *When it Comes* (BBC Radio Wales).

Matthew Pidgeon
(Mullet; Minstrel)

Matthew Pidgeon was born in the USA and trained at the RSAMD. His theatre credits include *The Wonderful World of Dissocia* (Tron Theatre, Drum Theatre & EIF); *The Lying Kind* (Royal Court); *Edward Gant's Amazing Feats of Loneliness* (Drum Theatre); *The Nest* (Traverse Theatre); and *8,000m* (Suspect Culture). His television credits include *Casualty*, *Taggart* and *Lee and Herring*; and films include *The Winslow Boy*, *State and Main*, *A Shot at Glory* and *Chopsticks*. His radio credits include *McLevy*, *Kaffir Lillies* and *The Holly and the Ivy*.

Note

For Anthony Neilson, Miriam Buether, Nick Powell and Chahine Yavroyan, please refer back to the biographies for *The Wonderful World of Dissocia*.

[NATIONAL THEATRE OF SCOTLAND]

The National Theatre of Scotland launched to the public on 25th February 2006 with its unique and defining opening event *Home*, which saw ten directors create ten pieces of work based on the theme of 'home' in ten different locations around the country. Since this flagship event, the National Theatre of Scotland and the audience response to it have re-invigorated my belief in the power of theatre to connect, to transform, to challenge and to transcend.

The National Theatre of Scotland has no building. Instead, we take theatre all over Scotland and beyond, working with existing venues and companies and, indeed, new spaces and companies, to tour and create theatre of the highest quality. Since we have no bricks-and mortar institutionalism to counter, all our money and energy is spent on creating our work. Our theatre really is without walls. It takes place in the great buildings of Scotland, but also in site-specific locations, community halls and drill halls, car parks and forests.

To date over 130,000 people have seen or participated in our work. We have produced 28 pieces of work in 62 locations from the Shetlands to Dumfries, and from Belfast to London. In our inaugural year, we took both the Edinburgh International Festival and the Fringe by storm, winning a clutch of awards including two Herald Angels, a South Bank Show Theatre Award, a Scotsman Fringe First, a Best Theatre Writing Award from The List and a Stage Award for Best Ensemble. In 2007/8, the international stage beckons, with tours to the USA and Australasia currently being finalised.

This season, along with *The Wonderful World of Dissocia*, we will embark on a UK tour of *Aalst*, in a co-production with Victoria and Tramway. The site-specific *Black Watch* will leave its Edinburgh home and tour all over Scotland, before a London residency as part of the Barbican's bite 07 Festival and a US tour. At the same time, *Tutti Frutti* will play in Glasgow, Edinburgh and Blackpool and *Futurology* (a co-production with Glasgow's Suspect Culture) will tour conference centres from Aberdeen to Brighton.

Meanwhile, our Young Company will be working with creative director Mark Murphy on *The Recovery Position* – a promenade piece designed specifically for their home at Platform in

Easterhouse, Glasgow. Our Learn department will be busy with their Transform and Connecting Communities events all over Scotland and will host their second youth theatre festival in Stirling. To mark the Highland Year of Culture, *Project Macbeth* will return for a special production in Elgin Cathedral, and summer will see the world premiere of *Venus as a Boy*, an NTS Workshop co-production with Burnt Goods based on Luke Sutherland's extraordinary novel.

Scottish theatre has always been for the people, led by great performances, great stories or great playwrights. The National Theatre of Scotland exists to build a new generation of theatre-goers as well as reinvigorating the existing ones; to create theatre on a national and international scale that is contemporary, confident and forward-looking; to bring together brilliant artists, designers, composers, choreographers and playwrights; and to exceed expectations of what and where theatre can be.

Vicky Featherstone, Artistic Director

For more information about
the National Theatre of Scotland, visit
www.nationaltheatrescotland.com
or call +44 (0) 141 221 0970

FOREWORD

I was at a low ebb at the start of the century. I'd been in a disastrous relationship with an impressionist and not the kind that paints. I'd just made a movie that had singularly failed to transform my life into a Hefnerian fantasy. I had a shit-load of stuff to write about but none of the objectivity required to make it interesting. I was homeless, completely broke and near-psychotic on amphetamines. I know – we've all been there. For the first time in fifteen years, I crawled home to Edinburgh where I intended to die, like a cat, under the bed.

Well, I didn't die, I just stopped taking so many drugs; which I've found to be a miracle cure for just about everything. But artistically I felt stale. The last successful play I'd written was *The Censor* (aka "that play where the woman takes a shit") and I wanted to do something different. At the time I was (as I periodically am) considered unemployable by most theatres and it was actually dear old Mark Ravenhill that got me out of that one by putting me onto the London Academy of Music and Dramatic Arts, where he'd just developed *Mother Clapp* with the students. With the help of new and old friends, I returned to London and LAMDA was where I first kicked around the ideas that would become *The Wonderful World of Dissocia*, and I owe a debt to everyone who was involved with that.

The next unshaven angels to hover into my life were Simon Stokes and David Prescott from the Theatre Royal Plymouth where I wrote a play called *Edward Gant's Amazing Feats of Loneliness*. It was the first overtly comedic play I had written since *The Night Before Christmas*, and I allowed my more fantastical imaginings full reign. It was a real liberation for me, the first trail of silver thread that just might take you somewhere new.

Next up was *Stitching*, which did pretty well and suddenly I was (as I periodically am) in demand again. Although ostensibly more akin to my older work in its imagery, I was pleased with its unconventional structure (easily understood by audiences, yet somehow mystifying to critics) and particularly with the inclusion of a dream sequence. It was very exciting to me that I could suddenly dip into a character's internal life without jarring the audience. I wanted to explore that further. But next was *The Lying Kind*.

Once you've heard an audience laugh, it's hard to go back. There was always humour in my earlier plays but it was pretty black; and that's the problem with black humour – when the lights go out you can't see it. So I had this crazy dream that maybe I could write a show for the Royal Court that would be on at Christmas and that would have no weightier purpose than to make the audience laugh. BIG mistake. Given that *The Lying Kind* was farcical in nature *and* on at the Court, I don't think there was one review that didn't compare me to Joe Orton (none of whose work I have ever seen) and find me lacking. My next commission for the Court was withdrawn. It would be four years until I had a show on in London again.

There were problems with *The Lying Kind* but I learnt a lot from doing it, and by the end of the run it was finding a very appreciative audience. It worked best with the kind of audiences that didn't frequent the Court very much; the kind of people who go to see a West End musical on special occasions.

I've always thought it very dangerous to dismiss populism. However cynical one may know some of the West End shows to be, there's no denying the audience's reaction to them. People are looking for something in theatre that they can't get anywhere else – a sense of live-ness, a certain spectacle. There's no part of me that needs to see *Chitty Chitty Bang Bang* on stage; but all of me wants to see that car fly. And that's what we've got to do, in the "serious" theatre – we've got to have our flying car. We've got to reclaim spectacle – the spectacle of ideas, of form, of passion. Audiences don't want to see what they can see on TV. We must be magical, or suffer the consequences.

Luckily I still had some believers outside London and once again, Plymouth came to the rescue. We went to Brian McMaster – then at the Edinburgh International Festival – and he agreed (with the Tron in Glasgow) to co-fund *Dissocia*, which I now felt ready to attempt.

I will presume that you know about the "In-yer-face" school of theatre, of which I was allegedly a proponent. I suppose it's better to be known for something than for nothing but I've never liked the term because it implies an attempt to repel an audience, which was never my aim. In fact, the use of morally contentious elements was always intended to do the very opposite. Given that one's genuine morality (as distinct from the morality that we choose for ourselves) tends to be instinctive rather than cerebral, engaging a receptive audience with such issues is a useful way of scrambling the intellectual responses that inhibit/protect us from full involvement with what we're watching. Engage the morality of an audience and they are driven into themselves. They become, in some small way, participants rather than voyeurs. That's why I prefer the term "experiential" theatre. If I make anything, let it be that.

Dissocia was a breakthrough for me in that (I believe) I managed to achieve with form what I had previously only achieved with content, in that the entire structure of the play was designed to force the audience into at least analogous identification with the protagonist, Lisa. Hopefully, when she is asked in the second act why she doesn't take the medication that will suppress the symptoms of her mental illness, the audience – having been deprived of the spectacle of the first half and of any conclusion to its narrative – will understand on a visceral level why she is drawn to her condition.

This harmony of form and content and the fact that I could legitimately employ music and songs and humour in the first half seemed to be a step further towards my personal grail: a truly theatrical theatre, intellectually accessible and satisfying to all, utilising populist methods to address serious subjects. I'm not implying that this is something new, just something rare.

Whereas *Dissocia* was partly an attempt to theatrically represent the internal landscape of someone who was mentally ill, *Realism* was an attempt to do the same for someone healthy. Though not, I think, quite as satisfying as *Dissocia*, the subject matter allowed me (almost) complete freedom to use music and humour, or to make drastic shifts in tone – whatever I felt was needed from moment to moment. It also allowed me to dramatise *contradiction*. A long held maxim has always been that drama differs from life because, in drama, you know what everyone wants. But that constant contradiction – the ability to both want and not want the same thing – is a fundamental part of the human character. In a regular narrative we embody these contradictions as opposing forces to the protagonist. It's the root of drama but it's also reductive. The greatest oppositional forces facing normal people come from within, and it was nice to find a way to portray that.

I'm telling you this just because it's the story of most writers, groping in the dark for new forms, better forms, getting knocked down, getting up again. I'm not sure if any of it means anything. I've long felt that the next movement in British theatre would be (for want of a better word) absurdist in nature. Caryl Churchill, David Greig and Martin Crimp have produced notable works in this style in recent years and there are many companies out there, both celebrated and not, to whom this is nothing new. The danger is that work of this type can easily become impenetrable. I will never believe it's right to send an audience out feeling confused and stupid. It's a needless failure of communication and it will be the death of theatre if it's encouraged. We must be accessible, yet still bold in form and content. The two are not contradictory. I suppose I'm humbly offering these two plays as evidence of that.

Thanks for reading. May all your cars fly.

Anthony Neilson, January 2007

The Wonderful World of Dissocia

Notes

What follows is a transcript of the original production of this play, including notes – where relevant – for translators. Stage directions, costume and design notes are therefore to be viewed as a guide only, and not as strict dictations. Nor, however, should they be dismissed out of hand. The set design, in particular, can be modified, but my advice would be to observe it to the extent that budget allows, as it is my belief that the overall concept serves the play well.

STAGE DESIGN

In Act One there is no scenery as such. Instead, the playing area is covered with domestic carpeting. Ideally, the stage should be raked. In venues with a proscenium arch it is suggested that the area in front of the safety curtain is also carpeted, that the first scene should be played in front of the curtain and that the curtain should be lifted after the elevator sequence, as Lisa enters Dissocia, to reveal the full expanse of carpet. This design concept is recommended for two reasons: firstly, it suggests that Act One is occurring in Lisa's 'interior'; secondly, such a large expanse of carpet mimics the view we have of the world in infancy – the hope being that the audience will be subconsciously more imaginative as a result.

COSTUME DESIGN

As the play begins, Lisa is meant to be going out somewhere with her boyfriend, so she would be wearing a party dress of some sort. This should be simple but bold in colour, indirectly suggesting the iconography of Dorothy's dress in the *The Wizard of Oz* or Alice's in *Alice in Wonderland*.

The emphasis in the first act is on colour, imagination and variety in all departments; but in costume terms this should be built up slowly. The elevator passengers will look quite normal; the Guards likewise, though one might begin to introduce some subtly odd elements. The first really outrageous costumes shouldn't appear until the Oathtaker team enters. This will serve to ease us into the world of Dissocia and maintain at least a tenuous link to the real world. In the 'Lost Property' sequence, Lisa is totally immersed and you can be as outrageous as you want (though you will find suggestions for costume in the stage directions).

SOUND DESIGN

The sound designer has two tasks in Act One: firstly, to help create the 'scenery' of Dissocia itself; secondly, to hint at what is actually happening in the real world. This 'real-life' narrative should only be suggested by occasional, subtle counterpoints to the action. A basic example is the 'elevator' scene – while Lisa perceives herself to be in a lift, the sound (and the actors' movements) suggest that she is actually in an underground train. Many other such possibilities exist, and will be suggested in the script where I feel them to be helpful.

In the original production, there was a continuous sound element in Act One, as a means of providing maximum contrast with Act Two. From the 'elevator' sequence on, stage microphones were used so we could give the actors' voices an unearthly quality, and also endow the stage space with a feeling of expansiveness.

In addition, there are three songs: 'Dissocia' was sung by the cast without accompaniment; 'What's an Hour' was sung by Lisa to a pre-recorded backing; and 'Who'll Hold Your Paw When You Die?' was pre-recorded. The chant of the Black Dog Army which ends Act One will be available on CD, but its use is entirely optional.

Characters

Lisa
Victor
Passenger 1
Passenger 2
Passenger 3
Passenger 4
Guard 1
Guard 2
Oathtaker
Oathtaker Attendants
Goat
Jane
Bear
Britney
Laughter
Ticket
Argument
Inhibitions
Biffer
Violinist
Nurse 1
Nurse 2
Nurse 3
Dr Clark
Dot
Dr Faraday
Vince

Act One

Lisa Jones – *a woman in her thirties* – *sits cross-legged onstage, absent-mindedly tuning the high E-string on an acoustic guitar.*

She tunes the string up and up until it reaches the correct note – and then continues on past it.

The pitch of the string rises and rises, but **Lisa***'s face remains blank, her eyes distant.*

Higher and higher the note, the string growing ever more taut, the fretboard beginning to tremble under the strain, the tension rising – but still she winds the tuning peg, up and up and up and up until . . .

. . . the string snaps!

. . . and lolls away from the fretboard.

Lisa *stares at it impassively, a child who has senselessly broken her toy.*

She gets up to put the guitar away. As she does so, someone rattles her letter box.

She stops in her tracks and listens.

Note: until his entrance, all **Victor***'s lines are either recorded or delivered, via mike, from offstage – a 'voice in her head'. The rattling letter box, however, is live.*

Victor Miss Jones?

The letter box rattles again. **Lisa** *remains still, fearful.*

Victor I know you're there, Miss Jones. I know you can hear me. It is vital that I speak to you.

The letter box rattles.

Please, Miss Jones. I have come a very long way to see you.

Lisa *doesn't know what to do.*

Lisa If it's money you want, I don't have any! You can take me to court and see how far it gets you!

Victor   I am not here for money, Miss Jones. I'm here to discuss your wristwatch.

Lisa *touches her wrist.*

Lisa   My . . . wristwatch?

Victor   You recently handed in a 1972 Sekonda wristwatch for repair . . .

She nods.

Lisa   It was going slow. They said it had to be sent to a specialist.

Victor   A specialist in Switzerland, yes; that is who I represent.

Pause.

I assure you, Miss Jones, it is very much in your interests to hear what I have to say.

Pause.

Lisa   You'd best come in then.

Lisa *lets* **Victor** *in. He bears more than a passing resemblance to how we imagine Sigmund Freud: goatee beard, long coat, gloves, walking stick, hat, pocket watch.*

Victor   Thank you, Miss Jones. Crouching at a letter box does little for the lower back.

Lisa   Have you come all the way from Switzerland?

Victor   There would be little point in coming only part of the way, don't you think?

Lisa   There's no need to be arsey. It's you that wanted to see me.

Victor   No. Forgive me; I am tired and I have . . . precision issues.

He presents **Lisa** *with his card.*

Victor   Victor Hesse. Of Hesse and Sons.

Lisa   Has something happened to my watch? You haven't
lost it, have you? It's just that my aunt passed it down to me
and –

Victor   Your watch is quite safe, I assure you. I wonder,
though – before I explain – could I possibly trouble you for
a small glass . . . ?

Lisa   Oh, yes, of course –

She is about to get him some water . . .

Victor   – of piss.

She stops.

Lisa   Of piss?

Victor   Yes – I drink a glass of urine every day. It's good for
the system .

Lisa   Really . . . ?

Victor   I haven't managed it yet, today. Contrary to popular
belief, it's not the sort of thing they serve on SwissAir.

Lisa (*reluctant to provide*)   I don't know . . .

Victor   You don't need?

Lisa   It's not so much that . . .

Victor   It's quite common. A lot of people do it.

Lisa   Well, yes, I've heard of it. It's just it's usually . . . their
own. That they drink.

Victor   Their own? I don't think so . . .

Lisa (*nods*)   Whenever I've heard of it.

Pause. For **Victor***, many things rattle into place.*

Lisa   I'm sorry, I just –

Victor   No: that does . . . make sense, now that you say it.
My brothers *have* been . . . unusually *supportive* of the habit.

Pause.

Well – on to business: my father's name is Sylvester Hesse.
Have you heard of him?

Lisa   I don't think so . . .

Victor   I'd be surprised if you had. We operate from a rather
remote Alpine location and our clientele is . . . exclusive, to say
the least. However, my father's work in the field of temporal
mechanics has been instrumental in the development of many
technologies – from the alarm clock to the internet.

Lisa   Do I have to pay extra for this? Because the man said
it'd be three, four pounds at the most or I'd just've –

Victor   This is not about money, Miss Jones. Your case is of
special interest to my father.

Lisa   But why, though? It's just a watch, isn't it?

Victor   To Sylvester Hesse there is no such thing as 'just a
watch'. Every clock face, every timepiece, reveals to him the
story of its owner; its hour hand mourns their losses, its minute
hand describes their lives, its second hand sings to him of
every moment spent in bliss.

Pause.

You don't believe me?

Lisa   I think you're exaggerating a bit . . .

Victor   No, Miss Jones, I am not! Quite the opposite. I know
how it sounds. But I have seen him *do* things; beautiful,
frightening, *maddening* things.

He sits down, cross-legged, on the floor and **Lisa** *joins him.*

Victor   When I was a child, my mother told me that he had
once made a watch so small, so ephemeral . . . that only a
butterfly could wear it. The notion delighted me but I did not
truly believe it. Until the day we found ourselves lost in the
woods and I saw him, Lisa – with these eyes that see you now –
I saw my father . . . take apart a spider . . . unspool its silk . . .
and reassemble the creature as a timepiece . . . powered by its
own tiny heart.

Lisa (*enchanted*)   That's impossible . . .

Victor   I cannot disagree. I only say that . . . I saw it.

He seems maudlin. **Lisa** *attempts to lighten the mood.*

Lisa   So he's fixed my watch, then?

Victor   Actually, no.

Lisa   No?

Victor   There was nothing to fix.

Lisa   It was going slow!

Victor   Was it?

Lisa   Yes – it was always an hour slow!

Victor   And you would reset it and wind it up but the next time you looked . . . ?

Lisa   It'd gone slow again.

Victor   And always by Exactly One Hour.

She nods.

Answer me honestly, Miss Jones: would you say that your life has recently been . . . out of balance?

Lisa   Well . . . it hasn't been great . . .

Victor   You've been finding it difficult to manage the . . . commitments of your life?

Lisa   I suppose.

Victor   You've become sluggish, unfocused, apathetic. You've neglected your friends, your family, your . . . relationship?

Lisa   But what's this got to do with my watch?

Victor   At the start of British Summer Time, the clocks go forward. You surrender an hour, correct?

She nods.

You surrender it in the belief that – when the clocks go back – this hour will be returned to you. However – in October last year – you returned from a trip to New York. British Airways Flight 771. Scheduled to depart at 12.05 but delayed by two hours. Of course, the time *here* is five hours ahead of the time *there*. But to complicate matters further, at the precise second you crossed the Greenwich meridian, the clocks here went back . . . by *exactly one hour*.

Lisa   So?

Victor   Think about it, Miss Jones! A seven-hour flight on BA from JFK with a two-hour delay on your UK ETA and a five-hour lag from EST to GMT just as BST is ending?!

She thinks about it.

Victor   You didn't get it back! Somehow, in all the temporal confusion of that instant, the hour that you surrendered – the hour that was rightfully yours – went astray! Do you see?

Pause.

Your watch is not an hour slow, Lisa, *you* are.

Over the next speech, lights narrow down on to **Lisa**. *A stage mike is used to add a hint of reverb to her voice. Strange, discordant sounds can be heard on the soundtrack.*

Lisa   Yes . . . yes, you know, that's right – I was really ill after that flight. And ever since, I've had this sort of . . . head cold, that I can't seem to shake off . . . And God, yes, you know it has been since then! Everything was OK before that trip to New York. But so . . . it's not me then, is it? I mean, it's not just me? This isn't just . . . how I am. Oh God and, you know, I *knew* that! I told them! Everyone's been giving me such a hard time about it – saying I don't care about anyone but myself, that I was just being lazy and miserable, but I wasn't! It wasn't my fault! I just lost an hour along the way!

Return to normal.

But, so – is there a way to get it back?

Victor   I am sure of it.

Lisa   And everything would be back . . . back to how it was?

Victor   Yes. If you reassimilate the hour, balance will be restored to your life.

Lisa   Balance will be restored to my life . . . God, you know, that's just like me to go losing an hour! I'd lose my head if it wasn't screwed on! So what do I have to do?

Victor   Your hour has been traced to a country called Dissocia. Arrangements have been made for you to travel there immediately. On the back of my card you will see a number. Once I have gone, you must dial it and follow the instructions you are given. When you arrive in Dissocia, you must make your quest known. Our agents will find you and assist you in your task.

Lisa   Wow . . . it's like being a spy or something!

Victor   This is no game, Miss Jones. A stray hour is a source of tremendous energy. In the wrong hands, its properties could be exploited to the most devastating ends. There are those who will not take kindly to your efforts to retrieve it; they will do what they can to obstruct you and mislead you.

He adopts the air of a hypnotist.

Just remember − the hour is yours. Never doubt it, never deny it. This will be your protection.

Lisa   I understand.

Victor   Good. The best of luck then, Lisa. My father is depending on you.

He exits.

Lisa *looks at the card. She takes out her mobile phone.*

Lisa   Balance will be restored to my life.

She dials the number. It rings, and then we hear an automated voice:

Automated Voice   Thank you for calling the Dissocian Embassy. If you wish to report a conspiracy, please press 1. If you think everyone would be better off without you, please press 2. If you wish to correct a temporal disturbance, please press 3. If you wish to press 4, please press 5.

Lisa *presses 3.*

Automated Voice   Thank you. You wish to correct a temporal disturbance. Your flat is now an elevator. To descend to Dissocia, please press 9.

Lisa   Balance will be restored to my life.

Decisively, she presses nine.

Immediately, there is a pinging sound.

From offstage, a voice:

Passenger 1   Hold the lift!

Lisa, *bewildered, has no idea how to do this.*

Suddenly (at least) four people have all cramped around her, as if in a small elevator. They look like fairly regular commuters.

Automated Voice   Doors closing. Going down.

The elevator begins its descent (although, curiously, it sounds more like an underground train).

Passenger 3 *makes a strange noise, like a groaning moose, but no one (save* **Lisa***) seems to notice. He does this a couple of times.*

Automated Voice   Going sideways.

Passenger 2 *takes out a mobile phone. She/he talks loudly and cheerfully:*

Passenger 2   Hi, it's me. Listen – I've been thinking about it, and I really think the easiest thing is to just push her down the stairs . . .

Lisa *can't believe what she's hearing.*

Passenger 2   Yeah. And I think you're right, she's almost bound to break her neck when she hits that landing. Yeah. And even if she doesn't, I think if you just prop her up and stamp on her chest . . . Exactly. I don't think anyone'll suspect us at all.

One of the **Passengers** *turns round to face a different direction. Slowly, the others do likewise.* **Lisa** *– thinking they must be turning to face the exit – does so too.*

Passenger 2   Exactly. Listen, I can't really talk about it now, I'm in a lift. What was that? Listen, I can't hear you, you're breaking up. I said you're breaking up. I'll see you tonight. Love you!

She puts the phone away.

Passenger 3 *groans.*

Automated Voice   Going down again.

Another **Passenger** *now turns back to the direction they were facing to begin with.* **Lisa***, getting a bit tired of all this, grudgingly follows.*

Passenger 3 *groans again, even more loudly than before.*

Lisa   Excuse me – are you all right?

This enquiry causes a ripple of disgust and embarrassment among the **Passengers***. They behave as if* **Lisa** *is mad.*

Lisa   What? I was just asking if he was all right – he was making that noise . . .

They try to ignore her. **Lisa** *sulks.*

Passenger 3 *groans again.*

Passenger 4 *– who has been reading a paper – turns to face sideways. Once again, the other* **Passengers** *follow.* **Lisa***, her arms folded, does not.*

A pinging sound.

Automated Voice   Dissocia. Arrivals.

Only now, as the doors open, does **Lisa** *turn. Just as abruptly, however, the* **Passengers** *about-face and leave the elevator in the opposite direction, leaving* **Lisa** *feeling stupid. Realising she should ask for directions,* **Lisa** *follows them –*

Lisa   Wait – excuse me! Excuse me – !

She follows the **Passengers** *offstage.*

By the ambient sound, the blinking lights and the airship that floats in the distance, it would seem that we are in some kind of airport arrivals lounge.

Two uniformed **Guards** *enter, mid-argument. They are both a mass of tics and twitches, bug-eyed and sweating with general paranoia.* **Guard 1** *is concerned about the length of his jacket.*

Guard 1   But does it cover my arse? Look –

Guard 2   Well, reasonably, I mean – most of it, yeah –

Guard 1   It only comes halfway down! You can see – there's such a steep drop from my arse to my legs – I've got such a fucking fat arse!

Guard 2   You haven't –

Guard 1   I have. It's womanly.

Guard 2   Womanly?!

Guard 1   Yeah, not so much fat as womanly –

Guard 2   There's nothing wrong with womanly!

Guard 1   Not on a woman, no, but on a man? It's grotesque! Men are meant to have small arses!

Guard 2   It looks fine, I'm telling you! I'd kill for an arse like yours: look at mine!

Lisa *is wandering around aimlessly when* **Guard 1** *sees her.*

Guard 1   Shit, look!

He grabs **Guard 2**, *stricken with fear.*

Guard 2   Bugger! And it's a woman too!

Guard 1   Should we go up to her?

Guard 2   We have to, don't we?! How do I look? Do I look terrible?!

Guard 1   No, you look fine – what about me? Does my breath smell?!

Guard 2   She's going to totally hate us!

Guard 1   I know – we're so fucking dull!

Lisa   Excuse me . . . . .

Guard 2   Um – hello – Um – can we help you?

He turns to **Guard 1**.

Guard 2   'Can we help you'! That's so fucking lame!

Guard 1   Yes, um – What we mean is – halt! Um – who goes there?!

Guard 2 *covers his face.*

Guard 2   Oh no . . . !

Guard 1   She thinks we're a right pair of twats!

Lisa   I just arrived, and I was wondering –

Guard 2   She's just arrived!

Guard 1   Oh – you mean you've just got here? (*To* **Guard 2**.) Of course she means that! What else would she mean?! I'm such a dick!

Lisa   I mean this is my first time here . . .

Guard 1   Ah, you mean you've never been here before!

He makes a 'duh' face at his own stupidity and immediately regrets it.

Shit, I shouldn't have made that face! I must've looked a right fucking prick! You do it!

He collapses to the ground. **Guard 2** *steps over him.*

Guard 2   Yes, sorry – you're saying you've never been here before?

Lisa   Not that I can remember.

Guard 2   Right. Because . . .

Guard 1   Because there are things . . .

Guard 2   There are things you have to do . . .

Guard 1   Things that *we* have to do . . .

Guard 2   Yes, to you –

Guard 1   Not *to* you, so much as –

Guard 2   – *with* you!

Guard 1   Exactly – *with* you –

Guard 2   There are things we have to do *with* you –

Guard 1   – if you haven't been here before.

Guard 2   Yes.

Pause.

Lisa   What sort of things?

Guard 1   Oh, it's nothing that bad, is it? I mean, it's not us, you understand –

Guard 2   No, I mean, we don't care –

Guard 1   We're quite easy-going, aren't we?

Guard 2   Yeah, I mean, we don't mind what anyone brings in, really –

Guard 1   No, I mean, as far as we're concerned you can bring in what you like, can't she?

Guard 2   Pretty much, yeah.

Guard 1   But, you know – the 'rules' say we've got to check, you know –

Guard 2   – that you're not, you know –

Guard 1   – bringing anything into the country that *we* wouldn't mind you bringing in –

Guard 2   – but that the *country* –

Guard 1   – that is, the *government* – um –

Both Guards   – would.

Lisa   It's all right, you know; I don't take it personally.

Guard 2   Are we boring you?

Guard 1   We are! We're boring her fucking rigid!

Lisa   No, really, you're not. I should think it's more boring for you.

Guard 2   Oh, it's not boring, is it?

Guard 1   Boring? No –

Guard 2   Not boring so much as –

Guard 1   – nerve-racking!

Guard 2   It's the war, you see.

Lisa   There's a war on?

Guard 1   There's always a war on.

Guard 2   We can't trust anyone. Not even a stranger like you.

Lisa   Oh dear. That must be awful for you.

Guard 1   Well, yes; but that is what we do.

Guard 2   Such is the lot . . . of an insecurity guard.

Pause.

Lisa   An *in*security guard?

Guard 2   Yes?

Lisa   Don't you mean a security guard?

The **Guards** *look at each other.*

Guard 2   What would be the point in that?

Guard 1   No, I mean, if it's *secure* –

Guard 2   – why would you have to guard it?!

Lisa   I suppose. (*Pause.*) Anyway, I don't want to be rude, but –

Guard 2   You want us to hurry up!

Lisa   I've just got something I have to find . . .

Guard 1   And you want us to get a bloody move on, of course you do! Of course she does!

Guard 2   You want us to stop dicking around like a couple of boring, ugly, fat-arsed pricks! Of course you do!

Lisa   What sort of things can I not bring in? You mean drugs, that sort of thing?

Guard 2   Drugs?!

Lisa   Yes, you know – heroin, cocaine, cannabis –

Guard 1   Oh goodness, no!

Guard 2   We take a stack of them every day!

Guard 1   Couldn't function without them!

Guard 2   No, no, it's other things . . .

Lisa   Like what?

The **Guards** *take out their notebooks.*

Guard 2   OK, well, do you have any . . . feathers?

Lisa   Feathers?

Guard 1   From a pillow or a bird, say.

Lisa   Why can't you bring in feathers?

Guard 1   Ah well, you see, a feather can be used to tickle a pilot's arse with –

Guard 2   Causing him to crash!

Lisa   I'm not getting on a plane.

Guard 1   But that's exactly what a pilot-tickler would say, isn't it?

Guard 2   Can't take any chances.

Lisa   Well, I don't have any feathers.

Guard 2   OK, well – have you got any . . . pants with –

Guard 1   Yes, with, like, clouds or – rabbits on them?

Lisa   What's the problem with that?

Guard 2   They can very easily be used to strangle pilots!

Guard 1   So easily.

Lisa   No, I don't have any pants with . . . clouds or rabbits on them.

Guard 1   Right. Good.

Guard 2   Well, we're whizzing through these, aren't we?! God, that sounded so *gay*!

Guard 1   What about – any heart-shaped pebbles?

Lisa   No.

Guard 2   Dolls' heads?

Lisa   No.

Guard 1   Tonto facsimiles?

Lisa   No. Whatever they are . . .

Guard 2   Gum shields? Stick insects? Flump covers?

'No' to each.

Guard 1   Buckaroo? Haunted House? Fuzzy Pumper? (*All board games that would have been popular in* **Lisa**'*s childhood.*)

Lisa   Nope.

Guard 2   Ping-pong tie-exfoliators?

Guard 1   She won't have one of *them*!

Guard 2   She might.

Offended, **Guard 2** *drags* **Guard 1** *aside.*

Guard 2   Don't undermine me!

Guard 1   I'm not!

Guard 2   You are! You're always undermining me!

Guard 1   What?! If anyone's being undermound round here, it's me!

Lisa *clears her throat.*

Guard 2   Sorry –

Guard 1 *throws himself around, like a child, at the injustice of it all.*

Guard 2   And no, like, really tiny houses or Knievel-shaped occupants . . . ?

Lisa   No.

Guard 2   And no donkey eggs?

Lisa   Definitely not.

Guard 2   All right – a couple of questions . . .

Guard 1   Has anybody other than yourself worn that dress today?

Lisa   Of course not.

Guard 1   OK – and have you left your hair unattended for any period of time or allowed anyone else to touch or stroke it recently?

Pause. For one fleeting moment, **Lisa** *seems sad.*

Lisa   No. No one.

The **Guards** *seem pleased with themselves.*

Guard 2   Well – I think we did pretty well there!

Guard 1   We did not bad.

Guard 2   We did OK.

Guard 1   We could have done better.

Guard 2   A lot better.

Guard 1   We made a total balls of it!

Guard 2   I was talking absolute shit!

Guard 1   I feel so fucking worthless!

Lisa   Well, listen – maybe you can help me. I'm looking for –

Guard 2   No, no, hold on – there's something else!

Guard 1   That's right! The oath!

Lisa   The oath?

Guard 1 *uses his walkie-talkie.*

Guard 1   Asshole 1 to control – this is Asshole 1. We need an Oath Team to Concourse 6 please. An Oath Team to Concourse 6 . . .

Guard 2   All new arrivals to Dissocia have to pledge allegiance to the Queen.

Lisa   You've got a Queen?!

Guard 2   Well, we did – sort of. I'm just telling her about the Queen.

Guard 1   Oh, right, yes.

Guard 2   You tell it better.

Guard 1   I so do not.

Guard 2   I always make an arse of it!

Guard 1   I'll start to cry if I tell it.

Lisa   Why, what happened?

Guard 1 *(tearful)*   Well, basically – we have a Queen . . . but she's missing.

Lisa   Oh dear . . .

Guard 2   Our Divine Queen has forsaken us!

Guard 1 *angrily grabs* **Guard 2** *by the lapels.*

Guard 1   She has not forsaken us! She is in hiding from the enemy! She'll return when it's safe to do so!

Guard 2 *puts up a fight.*

Guard 2   And when will that be, eh? When will it be safe?!

They wrestle each other to the ground.

Guard 1   Never!

Guard 2   It'll never be safe, ever!

Lisa *tries to intervene.*

Lisa   Safe from who?

Then there is the sound of a drum, and the two **Guards** *stop struggling, their mood suddenly changed.*

Guard 1   Oh, never mind that! It's the Oathtaker!

An imposing figure – the **Oathtaker** *– appears, comically grim, in robes and a ridiculous ceremonial wig. He has a round biscuit in one hand, and is attended by four ceremonial* **Attendants**.

Of the two **Attendants** *directly behind him, one carries an empty tray; the other carries a tray with a glass of water on it. Of the two behind them, one wears a drum; the other wears finger-cymbals.*

As the procession takes a step, the **Oathtaker** *intones these words in solemn fashion:*

Oathtaker   Oath-taker.

This is followed by a single beat of the drum.

On the next step, as one, his **Attendants** *reply:*

Attendants   Oatcake-eater.

As they do, the **Oathtaker** *takes a bite from the biscuit that he carries.*

This is followed by a single clash of the finger-cymbals.

And so it goes on, as they approach.

Oathtaker   Oath-taker.

Drum.

Attendants   Oatcake-eater.

Cymbal.

Oathtaker   Oath-taker.

Drum.

Attendants   Oatcake-eater.

Cymbal.

The **Oathtaker** *stops the procession for a moment and beckons his tray-carrying* **Attendants***. The one with the glass of water steps up and kneels beside him. The* **Oathtaker** *lifts the glass from the tray and takes a drink of water. He clears his throat and returns the glass. The tray-carrying* **Attendants** *return to their original positions, and then it begins again:*

Oathtaker   Oath-taker.

Drum.

Attendants   Oatcake-eater.

Cymbal.

And so on, until they arrive at **Lisa** *and the* **Guards***.*

The **Oathtaker** *beckons his tray-carrying* **Attendants***. The one with the empty tray steps up and kneels beside him.*

The **Oathtaker** *throws the biscuit down, and the* **Attendant** *returns to position.*

The **Guards** *position* **Lisa** *in front of the* **Oathtaker***.*

Guard 2   Right – you stand there.

Lisa   Is this really necessary? I don't think I'll be here that long.

Guard 1   Look at her! She looks beautiful, doesn't she? You look beautiful!

Guard 2   I always cry at oath-takings!

Oathtaker   Will them that wants the oath taken step forward.

The **Guards** *prod* **Lisa** *forwards.*

Lisa   Um – yes, sir – that's me.

Oathtaker   Raise your wrong hand.

Lisa   My wrong hand?

Oathtaker   Sorry, your *right* hand.

She does so.

Now – repeat after me: I –

Lisa   I.

Oathtaker   And state your full name.

Lisa   Lisa Montgomery Jones.

Oathtaker   Lisa Montgomery Jones.

Pause.

Yes?

Lisa   It's you.

Oathtaker   Eh?

Lisa   It's you that's telling me.

Oathtaker   Is it?

Pause.

Where were we?

Lisa   I, Lisa Montgomery Jones –

Oathtaker (*nods*)   I, Lisa Montgomery Jones –

Pause.

Yes?

Lisa   It's you again. You're the Oathtaker.

Attendants   Oatcake-eater!

*The tray-carrying **Attendants** step up and kneel beside him.*

*Annoyed, the **Oathtaker** hurriedly takes a bite of the biscuit and follows it with a drink of water.*

*It catches in his throat, and he coughs and splutters for a while. His **Attendants** pat his back until he recovers.*

Oathtaker   Now – where were we?

Lisa   I, Lisa Montgomery Jones –

Oathtaker   Do hereby swear –

Lisa   Do hereby swear –

Oathtaker   My undying –

Lisa   My undying –

Oathtaker   Allegiance –

Lisa   Allegiance –

Oathtaker   To –

Lisa   To –

Oathtaker   Our –

Lisa   Our –

Oathtaker   Divine Queen Sarah –

Lisa   Divine Queen Sarah –

Oathtaker   Of the House of Tonin –

Lisa   Of the House of Tonin –

Oathtaker   Of the House of Tonin –

Lisa   Of the House of Tonin –

Oathtaker   Of the House of –

Lisa   Have you got lost again?

Oathtaker   No, no; they've got three houses.

Lisa   Of the House of Tonin –

Oathtaker   Sovereign of the East Wing of the Divided States of Dissocia –

Lisa   Sovereign of the . . . East Wing . . . of the Divided States of Dissocia –

Oathtaker   And pledge, in her absence –

Lisa   And pledge, in her absence –

Oathtaker   To defend her dominion –

Lisa   To defend her dominion –

Oathtaker   From the armies . . . of the Black Dog.

Lisa   From the –

*But everyone (except the **Oathtaker**) puts one hand on the top of their head, bows and murmurs this phrase:*

Guards/Attendants   Queen Sarah, protect us from the Black Dog King!

Pause.

Lisa   From the armies of the Black Dog –

They all repeat the action:

Guards/Attendants   Queen Sarah, protect us from the Black Dog King!

Oathtaker   And –

Lisa   And –

Oathtaker   In –

Lisa   In –

Oathtaker   So –

Lisa*'s beginning to get annoyed.*

Lisa   So –

Oathtaker   Doing –

Lisa *(sighs)*   Doing –

Oathtaker   Hereby make enemies of any other enemies, however many, if any, amen.

Pause.

Lisa   Hereby make enemies . . . of any . . . other enemies?

She turns to the **Guards**, *who mouth the words.*

Lisa   However many – if any – amen!

The **Guards** *applaud.*

Oathtaker   And now for the Ceremonial Song!

They all launch into the song 'Dissocia'.

All
Welcome to Dissocia
We're so pleased to meet both of ya
We already feel close to ya
Dissocia, Dissocia!

And though we'd never boast to ya
We'll be such damn good hosts to ya
We'll even make a roast for ya
Dissocia, Dissocia!

And now you are our friend we will
Defend you to the end remember
No one in the world above will
Love you like the people of
This wonderful new world.

And so we raise a toast to ya
We'll even give the vote to ya
We'll forward all your post to ya
Dissocia!

Lisa *ends up on one of the* **Guard**'s *shoulders, as cannons blast streamers all over her, the Dissocians arrayed around her Broadway-style. The jollity ends quite abruptly.*

Oathtaker   Right. I'm off for a shit.

But suddenly a siren starts up, and a mechanised voice:

Mechanised Voice   Incoming attack – assume safety posture! Incoming attack – assume safety posture!

Everyone starts running around in a panic, stuffing pieces of material into their mouths.

Lisa What's going on?!

Guard 1 *tears a strip of material in two and hands her a piece.*

Guard 1 Put this between your teeth and bite down on it!

Lisa What?!

Guard 1 Do it!

She does it. Everyone is lying down, the gags in their mouths, clutching the tops of their heads. The siren is deafening. **Lisa** *lies down.*

Guard 2 Press down on the top of your head!

But his voice is muffled by the gag, and **Lisa** *can't hear him. He pulls the gag out of his mouth.*

Guard 2 Press down hard on the top of your head! Don't let go until –

And then it hits: a wave of low-frequency sound that can be felt rather than heard. It's almost peaceful – like the silence between the detonation of a bomb and the blast itself.

The Dissocians seem to be in a state of seizure, their mouths crooked, their ears and noses bleeding. Some of them lose control of their bladders.

Guard 2 *– caught without his gag in – is bleeding from the mouth.*

Lisa *crawls over to him. Keeping one hand on her head, she manages to put the gag back in his mouth.*

And then, a huge and frightening voice seems to form out of the rumbling:

Voice
   Citizens of Dissocia!
   Surrender your Queen
   Or live forever in the fist
   Of the Black Dog King!

And then, abruptly, the attack ends.

Mechanised Voice The attack is over – resume your business. The attack is over – resume your business.

Groaning, the Dissocians begin to pick themselves up.

Lisa   What on earth was that?!

Guard 1   It's happening every day now!

Lisa   I thought my head was going to explode . . .

Guard 2   It would've, if you hadn't been holding it down.

Lisa   But who was that voice?

Guard 1   That was him –

Guard 2   The Black Dog King!

Those within earshot cover their heads and repeat the mantra:

All   Queen Sarah, protect us from the Black Dog King!

Guard 2   Oh, I don't know why we bother with that! Queen Sarah's not going to save us! She's as scared as we are!

Guard 1   Keep your voice down!

Guard 2   Well, where is she then?! If she loves us so much, why hasn't she come back?! Why doesn't she do something?!

Guard 1   You know why! As long as she's alive, there's hope!

Guard 2   And how would we know?! Nobody even remembers what she looks like! For all we know, she could have been dead for years!

Suddenly, the **Oathtaker** *is there, in a fury.*

Oathtaker   Shut your blasphemous hole, boy! How dare you speak that way of your Queen?!

Guard 1   He's sorry, Oathtaker. He's just a bit tired, aren't you?

Oathtaker   We're all tired! But the very fact that he is able to speak such blasphemy is proof that our Queen still lives! And when the time is right, she will return to save us all!

Guard 2   Forgive me, Oathtaker.

Oathtaker   Take heed then. For if I hear such slander from you again, you'll be up before the Collective!

Guard 2   Yes, Oathtaker.

*The **Oathtaker** and his **Attendants** exit.*

Lisa *approaches the **Guards**, still nursing their injuries.*

Lisa   He's a bit scary . . .

Guard 2   He hates my guts!

Guard 1   No he doesn't. If he hates anyone, it's me.

Guard 2   You're joking, aren't you? He loves you! You even get invited to his Twister evenings!

Guard 1   Only because I've got a new mat!

Lisa   Listen – I need to ask you something . . .

Guard 2   We probably won't know the answer. But you can try.

Lisa   OK, well, you see – I actually came here – to find something. Something I've lost.

Guard 1   Oh yes?

Guard 2   And what would that be?

Lisa   Well, it's . . . an hour. My hour, actually. I lost it.

*The **Guards** freeze in terror, staring at each other.*

Guard 2   An hour!

Guard 1   She's lost an hour!

Lisa   I know it sounds a bit odd but I was told it was here. I just don't know where . . .

Guard 1   Ah, right, yes, well –

Guard 2   An hour, yes –

Guard 1   Well, that's probably, that's probably – um –

Guard 2   I know!

Guard 1   Do you?

Guard 2   Yes – Lost Property!

Guard 1   Lost Property, of course!

Guard 2   It's the very place!

Lisa   So where's that? In here?

Pause. The **Guards** *seem confused.*

Guard 1   *In* here?

Only then does **Lisa** *realise that they are now outside. There are birds singing.*

Lisa   Oh. That's funny.

Pause.

Guard 1   OK, then. Bye!

Guard 2   Bye!

They almost fall over each other trying to get away, but **Lisa** *stops them.*

Lisa   You haven't told me how to get there!

Guard 1   Where?

Lisa   Lost Property.

Guard 1   Oh, right, yes. How does she get there?

Guard 2   How − ? Oh, yes, well − follow the sun?

Guard 1   That's right. Just − follow the sun and you'll get there.

Lisa *looks in the direction of the sun.*

Lisa   But it's setting . . . ?

Guard 1   No, it's set.

Guard 2   That's how it set −

Guard 1   Setting.

Lisa   Oh. All right, well − thank you. It was nice to meet you.

She shakes their hands (strangely, as during the song 'Dissocia', they also shake the hand of someone we can't see).

And I don't think you should be so insecure. You both seem like lovely people.

Sheepishly, they nod their thanks.

Guard 2   Be careful, won't you?

Lisa   I will.

Guard 1   Don't talk to strangers.

Lisa   I'll try not to. Bye.

They watch her walk off towards the setting sun. **Lisa** *exits.*

Guard 2   Did we do the right thing?

Guard 1   We did what we were told.

Guard 2   We're such fucking lackeys.

Guard 1 (*nods*)   We're pricks.

They exit.

Lisa *re-enters, the sun in her eyes. She sings to herself:*

Lisa
Dissocia, Dissocia
We're dum dum dum dum dum da ya
We'll even roast a goat for ya
Dissocia, Dissocia . . . . .

She comes to a stop.

Follow the sun. But it's just fields. Why would they have Lost Property in the middle of a field? That's the problem with insecure people; they just tell you what you want to hear.

Pause.

It does make for a beautiful sky, though, when the sun sets setting.

Pause. She has an idea: she takes out her mobile phone and dials a number. To her surprise, it works. (Here we might hear an effect similar to that outlined on page 10.)

Vince, it's me. Listen – I know I was supposed to be seeing you tonight and you probably think I'm messing you around, but something really important's come up. You know how I've been acting a bit funny recently? Well, it's because I lost an hour on the way back from New York. So you see, it isn't just me; I *do* know what love is and I *do* care about people. Anyway, my flat turned into an elevator and I've gone to this place called Dissocia. It's quite an odd place but the people are nice and the sky is really colourful and hopefully I'll be back soon with balance fully restored so don't worry about me. Give me a ring when you get this. Bye.

She puts the phone away. Pause.

I suppose that sounds a bit weird. I mean, it doesn't sound very much, an hour. Losing a year of your life, that's impressive – but an hour? I mean . . . what's an hour?

She makes a gesture as she says this:

An hour is just a sixty-second cycle –

She stops. A musical phrase has played under this.

Pause. She repeats the action:

An hour is –

The musical phrase occurs again. It seems to be connected to the gesture.

She makes the gesture on its own and, again, the musical phrase.

Obviously, this is a musical field. She giggles.

She makes a gesture like an orchestra conductor and the musical phrase plays again, in a classical style. This is not what she wants.

She thinks.

She makes a sexier gesture and the musical phrase plays again, in a swing style.

She shakes her head. She thinks. She decides.

Sweeping her arms up in a gentler motion, it's as if she lifts the music up from the ground, like flowers.

She sings 'What's an Hour'.

An hour is a sixty-second cycle
Dictated by our journey round the Sun
It's frequently divided into quarters
Like the hash we used to buy from Davy Dunn.
An hour is a twenty-fourth of daytime
If life's a bitch, an hour is a flea
An hour doesn't mean
So very much in itself
But it's my hour
And it means a lot
To me.

Of course I know an hour is just a construct
Concocted by an order-hungry race
I'm familiar with the work of Stephen Hawking
(Though I'm not sure I would recognise his face).
We could sit here and debate the implications
Until our faces turned a funny shade of blue
An hour is simply three thousand
Six hundred seconds
That I
Could have spent
With you.

An hour is simply three thousand
Six hundred seconds
That I
Should have spent
With you.

Lisa *laughs, looking skywards, and a flurry of petals falls around her.*

She crouches down to play with them, but the petals become flies, which buzz around her. She runs away from them.

Lisa   Go away! I hate flies! Go away!

But they persist, clustering around her bottom.

What are you doing around my arse?! You know that's very insulting! These pants were clean on this morning!

Goat   They're timeflies.

*A **Goat** is tethered nearby.*

Lisa   What?

Goat   Timeflies. Haven't you heard of them?

Lisa   Timeflies? Not really.

Goat   Never?

Lisa   Well, apart from as part of a phrase – 'Time flies when you're having fun.' I've heard that.

Goat   There you are, then.

Lisa   'Time flies when you're having fun'?

Goat   'Tend to cluster round your bum.'

Lisa   I've never heard that bit before.

Goat   And that's my fault, is it?

Lisa   No . . .

Goat   That's what you're implying.

Lisa   No, it's not.

*The **Goat** shrugs. Pause.*

Goat   They've gone now anyway.

Lisa *nods. The timeflies have, indeed, gone.*

Goat   That's because you're not having fun.

Lisa   If you say so.

Goat   I suppose that's my fault as well.

Lisa   Why would it be your fault?

Goat   It stands to reason: you were having fun – hence the timeflies – and then you met me, and now you're not. So it's obviously my fault.

Lisa   No, really, it isn't. I wasn't even having that much fun to begin with.

Goat   But you're having less now.

Lisa   Well . . .

Goat   And you're blaming me for it. You can, you know; it's all right.

Lisa   I don't want to blame you.

Goat   But I'm to blame.

Lisa   You're really not –

Goat   I am! I am to blame, I am!

The **Goat** *is very upset.* **Lisa** *sits beside him.*

Lisa   Oh no, what's wrong? Why are you crying?

Goat   I'm a miserable failure!

Lisa   Why are you saying that? How are you a failure?

Goat   Nobody ever blames me for anything! What's the point in being a scapegoat if you never get blamed for anything?!

Lisa   Oh . . . you're a *scapegoat*.

Goat   Isn't it obvious?

Lisa   Not really. I mean, you're obviously a goat . . .

Goat (*nods*)   But not obviously a scapegoat. I know. That's half the problem; people can't see the difference. And they're not likely to go around blaming ordinary goats for things. That'd be ridiculous; not to mention unfair.

Lisa   So you *want* me to blame you?

He nods.

But you really weren't to blame . . .

Goat   But that's good! There's no point in blaming me for things I'm to blame for. Anyone can be blamed for things they're to blame for. A scapegoat is blamed for things they had little, or nothing, to do with.

Lisa   Oh. Well, I suppose I could blame you for something . . .

Goat Could you?

Lisa If it'd make you feel better . . .

Goat Oh, it would!

Lisa All right, well . . .

Goat Make it something big. Something that really upset you.

Lisa OK –

She clears her throat and adopts a mock-angry tone.

Why did you put that mortice lock on? You know I lost my key! I had to sit outside for three hours until Mrs Cameron came back and it was really cold and raining!

Pause.

How was that?

Goat I said something that really upset you.

Lisa It did upset me! I was furious!

Goat But something big though!

Lisa Big like what?

Goat How about your childhood? You could blame me for that.

Pause.

Lisa There's nothing to blame you for.

Goat Nothing?

Lisa I had a very happy childhood, thank you. I was a very happy little girl.

[In the original production, the second sentence was also pre-recorded and played simultaneously to the actor speaking the line.]

Goat *(shrugs)* If you say so.

Pause.

Lisa   This is stupid. I can't blame you for something I know you didn't do.

Goat   What about something I *might* have done?

Lisa   How d'you mean?

Goat   Well – something *somebody* did . . . but you don't know who. Something I could *possibly* have done – for all you know.

Lisa   Oh, yes, all right – Give me back my purse!

Goat   Eh?

Lisa   You stole my purse! You took it out of my bag in the cinema!

Goat   Did I fuck!

Lisa   Yes, you did! There wasn't even anything worth having in it – just a picture of my auntie and that was the only one I had, you sod!

Goat   I never stole your fucking purse! I've never even *been* to a fucking cinema!

Lisa   So you're going to deny it?

Goat   Of course I am! I didn't do it!

Pause. **Lisa** *doesn't understand.*

Lisa   Well, I know / you didn't, but –

Goat   But you don't know that for a fact! I *might* have done it – !

Lisa   Oh, I'm sure I'd have noticed a goat in the cinema!

He starts to cry again.

Goat   I thought you were trying to make me feel better!

Lisa   I know, I'm sorry.

Goat   It's not your fault. It's this war we're having. Everybody just blames the enemy for everything. There's nothing for a scapegoat to do!

Lisa *is at a loss. Then she has an idea.*

Lisa   Oh, wait a minute, of course, it's perfect! You stole my hour!

Slowly, the **Goat** *raises his head.*

Goat   What did you say?

Lisa   Well, I lost an hour, you see; that's why I'm here. But I reckon you stole it, you . . . thieving . . . goat, you! Give me back my hour!

The **Goat** *stands.*

Goat   Wait, wait – I wasn't ready. But that was good –

Lisa   Was it?

The **Goat** *positions* **Lisa** *so she's facing front. She doesn't understand why, but goes along with it.*

Goat   Yes, blame me for that. Blame me for the hour.

The **Goat** *pulls free the rope he was tethered with, and gathers it up.*

Lisa   All right – ready?

He stands poised behind **Lisa**.

Goat   Ready.

Lisa   Give me back my – !

Suddenly, the **Goat** *ensnares her with the rope.*

Goat   I've found her, Master! She's here! The girl that seeks the hour!

Lisa   What are you doing?! Let me go! You're hurting me!

She tries to pull away, but the **Goat** *has the rope firmly and starts to reel her in.*

Goat   I've got no choice, don't you see? He'll have to let me join him now.

Lisa   Who will? Join who?

Goat   The Master! He who will bring calamity to Dissocia! The Destroyer! The Black Dog King!

The sound of distant thunder.

Having reeled **Lisa** *in, the* **Goat** *winds the rope around her and ties it tight.*

Lisa   Listen, please – I really think you're making a mistake. I've never even been here before!

Goat   There's no mistake! A girl will come seeking an hour – she must be found! Oh, and I'll be rewarded with a lifetime of blame! I'll be the greatest scapegoat that ever lived!

He forces **Lisa** *to the ground and dances around her, in glee.*

Goat
    Rivers of bile will vein the land!
    Bones will twist inside the hand!
    Children will boil in mothers' wombs!
    Turning on lights will darken rooms!
    And heavy skies will teem with flocks
    Of tiny birds with human cocks!

Lisa   This is really horrible of you! And after all the things I tried to blame you for!

The sound of passing cars, as if we're on a motorway lay-by.

The **Goat** *has become distracted by the sight of* **Lisa**'s *bottom, as she struggles.*

He looks around, furtively. Decisively, he turns her over.

Lisa   What are you doing?

With one final glance behind him, the **Goat** *hitches up her dress.*

Goat   Just be quiet and you might enjoy yourself!

He starts to undo his trousers.

Lisa   Oh my God, what are you doing?!

The traffic is deafening now. The **Goat** *grunts as he tries to enter her.*

Lisa *lets out a shrill and chilling scream . . .*

And then, suddenly –

– the 'toot-toot' of a horn!

The **Goat** *stops what he's doing.*

A woman drives on in a child's pedal car. She comes to a stop right beside them.

Jane   Hello there!

Jane *is dressed like a secretary, but she also wears an eyepatch, has one of her arms in a sling, and has a support bandage on her leg: she's in bad shape, but she covers it well with make-up and a thoroughly cheerful demeanour. She is one of those people whose sentences rise at the end, like questions.*

My name's Jane and I'm from the CCS – the VCI – the CV – ? I'm from the Council.

Goat   I know where you're from.

Jane *consults her clipboard.*

Jane   Now – which one of you is Miss Lisa Montgomery Jones?

Lisa   Me! That's me, here.

Jane   Right – do you think you could maybe just untie Miss Jones for me?

The **Goat** *unties* **Lisa**.

Jane   All right, Miss Jones – Could you just confirm for me your date of birth?

Lisa   Um – 17th June 1969. (*Or as appropriate.*)

Jane   Right; and you've been a citizen of Dissocia for how long?

Lisa   Just a few hours really.

Now free, **Lisa** *tries for a kick at the* **Goat**, *who dodges it.*

Jane   A few hours. OK.

She notes this down.

So I take it you're Gavin Loxley?

The **Goat** *nods.*

Jane   And you're how old?

Goat   Six.

Lisa   Six?!

He nods.

You're a very, very, *very* bad goat!

Jane   Well, that all seems to be in order. D'you think you could just – help me out of this car?

Lisa *takes her arm.* **Jane** *shouts in pain.*

Jane   Not the arm, not the arm!

Lisa   Oh, I'm sorry –

She takes **Jane**'*s hand and helps her out.*

Jane   Anyway, as I said, my name is Jane? I'm from the Community Crime Initiative?

Lisa *nods.*

Jane   And I'm here to be beaten and anally raped for you.

Pause.

Lisa   You're what?

Jane   Right, well, what it is? Is what we call the Victim Concentration Scheme. Which is basically that Mr Loxley here was going to beat and anally rape you –

Lisa   He was what?!

Goat   I was going to piss on her as well.

Jane   Were you?

She looks at her clipboard.

Lisa   You dirty little sod!

Jane   Oh, I *am* sorry. It's been one of those days today.

She scrubs it out.

Right, so anyway; he was going to beat, anally rape and urinate on you –

Lisa (*shakes head*)   I can't believe that! I thought you just took the blame for things?

Goat (*shrugs*)   There's no smoke without fire.

Jane   But I'm here to be BAU'd on your behalf.

Lisa   Why would you want to do that?

Jane   Right, well, what it is? Is that under the previous Council? This borough had actually the highest crime rate in Dissocia. For example, over the last year, there were an average of *twenty-two* serious crimes per week.

Lisa   How many are there now?

Jane   Under the new scheme?

Lisa *nods.*

Jane   *Forty*-two.

Pause.

Lisa   So it's doubled?

Jane   Right, well, whilst it's true to say that, since the scheme began, statistics do show that serious crimes have increased – ?

Lisa   Doubled.

Jane   Doubled, yes, that's true, but actually what they don't tell you? Is that the number of *individual victims* of crime has, in fact, *fallen*?

Lisa   Fallen?

Jane   Yes, well, under the last administration? There was an average of *twelve hundred* individual victims of crime per year.

Lisa   And how many are there now?

Jane   Under the new scheme?

Lisa   Yes.

Jane   One.

Lisa   One?

Jane *suddenly gets a stabbing pain in her side.*

Jane   One!

She grabs hold of **Lisa** *as the pain passes.*

Lisa   And that's you.

Jane   And that's me.

Goat   I certainly feel a lot safer than I used to.

Jane   So – shall we crack on with it, then?

Jane *hobbles to her pedal car. The* **Goat** *follows.*

Lisa   Wait a minute – I don't want you to get beaten and raped in my place!

Jane   Right, well; the only alternative would be for it to happen to you. And I don't think you'd want that. OK?

She takes a medical kit out of the car, and starts to pull on a pair of surgical gloves.

Lisa   But how's that the only alternative? I mean, you've stopped a crime. Why does it have to happen at all?

Pause. **Jane** *can't think of an answer to that.*

Jane   Right, well, I'm not actually in the position of deciding Council Policy? I'm just the victim. Mr Loxley?

She beckons to the **Goat***, who follows her offstage.*

Lisa   No, listen, this is ridiculous, please –

She grabs the end of the **Goat***'s rope.*

Lisa   This is really stupid! Please don't do this! You're only six and it's a really wicked thing to do!

With a grunt, he pulls it free and exits.

Helplessly, **Lisa** *watches the offstage action: there is the sound of animal grunting,* **Jane** *screaming, the sound of blows.*

Lisa *can't watch any more.*

The awful sounds build and build.

(Note: in the original production, the live offstage sounds were eventually swamped by a treated recording of a violent domestic argument.)

Lisa *covers her ears and sings to herself:*

Lisa
    Dissocia, Dissocia! We'll even make a boat for ya!
    We'll dum dum dum dum dum for ya! Dissocia Dissocia!

She runs back and screams at them:

Leave her alone, d'you hear me? What's she ever done to you?! Leave her alone, you rotten horrible goat!

But the noise just gets louder. She starts to cry.

I hate this place, I hate it! I hate it and I want to go home! I want to go home! I want to go home!

She lies down and curls up, in a foetal position, her ears covered.

I want to go home I want to go home I want to go home.

Dissocia darkens around her, and the violent noises recede until finally she is just a small, lonely figure in the landscape. She makes little bleating pre-linguistic sounds.

Pause.

A trapdoor opens near her head, hissing out icy smoke. A **Polar Bear** *clambers out.*

When **Lisa** *sees him, she smiles.*

Bear   Hello, Lisa.

Lisa   Hello, bear. How are you?

Bear   Mmm. Not so bad.

Lisa   What've you got for me?

Bear   I've written a song.

Lisa   Have you?

Bear   Would you like to hear it?

Lisa   I would. I'd very much like to hear it. Is it nice?

Bear   It's quite nice, yes. Shall I begin?

Lisa   Please do.

The **Bear** *clears his throat. He sings 'Who'll Hold Your Paw When You Die?'*

Who'll hold your paw when you die?
Who'll hear you whisper goodbye?
Who'll be beside you when brain death is declared?
Who'll think about you and all we have shared?
Some people call themselves friend
But will they be there when you end?
Life's full of clatter
But none of it matters
Only who'll hold your paw when you die.

Delighted, **Lisa** *applauds.*

Lisa   That was excellent!

Bear   It's not really finished yet.

Lisa   It was very good though.

Bear   Hmm. Thank you. D'you feel better now?

Lisa   I do. I really do. You've restored my faith in animals.

Bear   All right then. See you then.

Lisa   Bye.

The **Bear** *disappears back into the ground.*

The light returns and, with it, the terrible sounds of the **Goat** *assaulting* **Jane**.

But now **Lisa** *is smiling, still enchanted by the* **Bear**'s *song.*

After a time, the noises end.

Jane *reappears, badly beaten up, her clothes torn, but still clutching her clipboard; and still thoroughly cheerful.*

Jane   All right?

Lisa   How are *you*?

Jane   Oh, I'm fine. I mean, a goat's penis – it's quite rough? But apart from that, I'm fine. So could you just sign here; just to say I've been raped and beaten for you?

Lisa *signs.*

Jane   And could you just date it for me? Thanks very much.

Lisa   No, thank *you*.

Jane   All right now, Mr Loxley is actually napping at the moment.

The sound of the **Goat** *snoring, offstage.*

Jane   But I believe he does still intend to hand you over to the enemy –

Lisa   I'm sure he's got that wrong. What would the Black Dog Thingummybob want with me?

Jane *puts her hand on her head.*

Jane   Queen Sarah protect us from the Black Dog Thingummybob.

Lisa   Unless it's my hour he wants. Victor did say it was a source of great power. Maybe he thinks I know where it is.

Jane   Right, well, I wouldn't know about that. But what I'd suggest? is that I give you a lift to Lost Property. Would that suit you?

Lisa   That would be fantastic!

Jane   Righty-ho.

Lisa *helps* **Jane** *to the car. But then something strikes her.*

Lisa   How did you know I was going there?

Jane   Beg your pardon?

Lisa   How did you know I was going to Lost Property?

Pause.

Jane   Because you told me?

Lisa   I don't think I did . . .

Jane   Mmm. Well, what it is – is it was probably Mr Loxley that told me? He was saying quite a lot of things as you can imagine.

Lisa *nods, not quite convinced.*

Jane   Anyway, we should probably go now? It's just that I'm due to be carjacked at six.

Lisa *climbs into the small car behind* **Jane**.

With a 'toot-toot', they drive off.

A sudden and thunderous blast of punky guitar music.

Jane *and* **Lisa** *are travelling at high speed around Dissocia's mountain roads.*

Lisa (*shouts*)   It's very fast this car, isn't it?!

Jane (*shouts*)   What?!

She turns down the music.

Lisa   I said it's very fast, this car!

Jane   What do you mean, car? It's not a car –

Jane *seems to have become someone entirely different.*

Lisa   Isn't it?

Jane   God, no!

Jane *pulls on a pair of goggles.*

Lisa   What is it, then, if it's not a – ?

Suddenly the car accelerates even faster, pressing them back into their seats.

– CAAAAAARRRRRR!

And then takes off into the sky, up and through the canopy of clouds.

She covers her eyes, terrified.

Oh no, listen, please – I'm not very good with flying and that's when I'm in a plane! Can we go back down, please?! Please can we go back down?!

Jane   Oh, nonsense: here, have a swig of this – that'll see you right.

Jane *swigs from a hip flask and passes it back.*

Lisa   Oh my God, you're drinking!

She looks over the side and screams.

Oh my God!

She takes the flask and drinks from it.

How is this thing flying? It doesn't even have any wings!

She looks down again – takes another swig.

Oh, we're so high up! – this is really . . .

But she continues to look (and continues to drink).

. . . quite beautiful. It's really quite beautiful!

Jane   What?!

Lisa   Dissocia – it's beautiful!

She whoops with joy.

It's *beautiful*!

She drinks from the hip flask again.

Jane   Yes, it is rather pretty, isn't it? The West was even prettier, once upon a time. But look up ahead!

Lisa   I think there's a storm brewing!

Jane   No – that's the West! The Black Dog reduced it to a wasteland in a matter of weeks! He'd do the same to us if he could!

Lisa   Why can't he?!

Jane   Because he wants Queen Sarah!

Lisa   But hasn't she gone missing?

Jane   Not exactly! The Collective sent her into hiding! Every single image of her was destroyed, even the money! Then they erased the memory of her face from every last citizen of Dissocia!

Lisa   So no one knows what she looks like?

Jane   Not a soul! So the Black Dog can't risk an all-out assault in case he kills her by accident!

Lisa   Here – you're not doing that thing! You know – Queen Sarah protect us – that thing.

Jane   Oh, that's just superstitious twaddle!

Lisa   You did it before!

Jane   I've never done it!

Lisa   You did, I saw you! After you were raped by the goat!

Jane   Have you gone fucking *mad*?!

Lisa   Don't shout at me – you were raped by a goat, I heard it!

Jane   It's hardly something I'd forget! Honestly, I don't know how you come up with these things, Lisa, I really don't.

[In the original production, the second sentence was also pre-recorded and played simultaneously with the actor speaking the line.]

An explosion goes off beside them, rocking the flying car.

Lisa   Oh my God, what's that?!

Another explosion.

Someone's shooting at us!

She looks over the side.

We're flying over the West!

Jane Yes, sorry about that! Just a little detour – have to drop something off!

Lisa What are you dropping off?

Jane A bomb.

Lisa A bomb?!

The air is filled with anti-aircraft fire and explosions.

Oh my God! We're going to die!

Jane Well – got to do our bit, haven't we?

Another explosion.

Lisa No, wait a minute – this isn't my bit, this is your bit! And anyway – I don't want to drop bombs on people, whatever they've done!

Jane No, no, no: this is a novelty bomb!

Lisa A novelty bomb?!

Explosion.

What the hell is a novelty bomb?! You mean, it doesn't kill anyone?

Jane Oh no – it incinerates everything in a five-mile radius!

Lisa So what's the novelty?

Jane It leaves a scorch mark in the shape of a cat! Here we go –

She pulls a lever.

Bombs away!

The bombs whistle to the ground. Beneath them, explosions mushroom.

Lisa   Oh my God! There's people burning!

Jane   Good! Take that, you big bullies!

Lisa   No, it's horrible – all the houses are burning, look – those are children down there!

Jane   Yes, but look at that!

Lisa   Oooh, you're right – it's a cat!

Jane   Quite good, isn't it?!

Lisa   Have you got any other ones?!

Jane   I've got one like a rhino?

Lisa   Oh, drop that one!

Jane *lets another bomb drop.*

Lisa   Wheeeeeeeeeeeee!

Another explosion beneath them. **Lisa** *looks back at it.*

That looks more like a walrus!

Jane   They're just prototypes. There's a good one that looks just like a little Scottie dog.

Lisa   Aww.

Simultaneously:

Jane   Die, you Black Dog scum!

Lisa   Die, you Black Dog . . . buggers!

More anti-aircraft fire on their tail.

Lisa *sits up and taunts them.*

Lisa   Come on, you want some?! You fucking want some?!

An explosion just behind them. **Lisa** *laughs.*

Jane   We're clear now!

Lisa   Well done! That was excellent!

Jane   You mustn't feel any sympathy for them, Lisa. They're all slaves to the Black Dog King!

Lisa   I hate the Black Dog King!

Jane   So you should! I dread to think what he'd have done if he'd caught you! I mean, you've heard that poem, haven't you?

They start their descent.

Lisa
Rivers of bile will vein the land?

Jane
Bones will twist inside the hand!

Lisa
Children will boil in mothers' wombs!

Jane
Turning on lights will darken rooms!

Lisa
And heavy skies will teem with flocks . . .

Both
Of tiny birds with human – cocks!

The car rattles as they contact the ground and taxi towards a halt.

Jane   That's the one! Have you ever seen a penis bird? Frightful things. Had one in the barn once. Came on my hand while I was saddling up.

Lisa   Eeeuh!

The car comes to a stop.

Jane   Anyway, here we are: Lost Property. Over that hill.

Lisa *climbs out.*

Lisa   Well, thanks so much for the . . . flight.

Jane   Not at all.

Lisa   I've never been on a bombing mission before. It was very exciting.

Jane   Yes, it is rather jolly, isn't it? Anyway – toodle-oo!

With a last 'toot-toot', **Jane** *drives off.*

Lisa *waves goodbye. She walks up the hill towards Lost Property.*

As she climbs to the top of the rake, the other actors will set up for the next section. **Lisa** *watches them do so, making gestures with her hands that recall the gestures she made in her solo song, as if she is in some way conjuring the events. Over this, the following pre-recorded conversation plays.*

The sound of traffic. A conversation on the move:

Vince (*voice-over*)   Lisa! Lisa – where have you been?!

Lisa (*voice-over*)   What do you mean, 'where've I been'?

Vince (*voice-over*)   I thought I was meant to be seeing you tonight.

Lisa (*voice-over*)   Were you?

Vince (*voice-over*)   So what were you doing at the fucking airport?!

Lisa (*voice-over*)   Just leave me alone, Vince.

Vince (*voice-over*)   Is that what you want? Do you really want me to leave you alone? Because I can do that. If that's what you want, I can do that. Because I'm telling you, I'm really getting fucking sick of this. Lisa, are you listening to me?!

Lisa (*voice-over*)   Do what you like.

A hot-dog stand, with a sign that reads 'Lost Property'. Behind the stand is a mound of shoes and handbags.

At the stand, a trashy-looking girl called **Britney** *is frying onions and splitting buns for the hot dogs.*

A muzak version of 'Who'll Hold Your Paw When You Die' is playing (or something similarly bland).

There are two outdoor café tables, with two people sitting at each. There are menus on the tables, showing nothing but hot dogs.

At table one sit two men we shall refer to as **Laughter** *and* **Ticket**. *They are respectably dressed.* **Ticket** *wears a panama hat. Every now and then* **Laughter** *will laugh loudly, and be hushed by* **Ticket**.

At table two sit another two men we shall refer to as **Argument** *and* **Inhibitions**. **Inhibitions** *wears a tweed suit and sports a bushy beard.* **Argument** *wears trousers and shoes – and no shirt, but a collar and bow tie, in the style favoured by male strippers.*

All of them are intently eating hot dogs from paper plates. There are no signs of water, or beverages of any kind.

Lisa *approaches* **Britney***, who is now putting hot dogs into rolls.*

Lisa   Um – hello. I wonder if you could help me? I've lost something.

Britney *sets off around the tables, giving out hot dogs.* **Lisa** *follows her as she weaves inbetween them.*

Britney   What do you want me to do about it?

Lisa   Well – it's Lost Property, isn't it?

Britney   If it's lost then, yes, obviously.

Lisa   No, I mean – *this* is Lost Property. Isn't it?

Britney   Does it look like Lost Property?

Lisa   No, not really. But the sign says it is.

Britney   The sign?

Lisa *indicates the sign.* **Britney** *stops to look at it. She sighs heavily.*

Britney   I'm surrounded by bloody idiots! Biffer!

Biffer *hurries in. He is a chef and wears a grimy apron. He is dripping with sweat and carrying a tray full of hot dogs.*

Britney   Biffer, get that bloody sign fixed! Give me those.

Biffer *gives her the hot dogs. He replaces the sign with one that reads 'Lost Lost Property'. And then hurries back to the kitchen.*

Lisa   '*Lost* Lost Property'?

Britney *has put more hot dogs, in buns, on more plates. She sets off round the tables again. Although they have more hot dogs than they can possibly eat, the men are never less than grateful.*

Britney   Yes, well, that's why I was confused. You're looking for the Lost Property Office.

Lisa   Where's that?

Britney   We lost it.

Lisa   You lost the Lost Property Office?

Britney   There's no need to rub it in! We're obviously embarrassed about it.

Lisa   So what do you do here?

Britney   Well, if anyone finds the Lost Property Office, they'll hopefully bring it to us.

Lisa   So what's all that stuff behind the stall?

Lisa *indicates the pile of shoes and handbags.*

Britney *picks up the ketchup and mustard bottles and goes round the tables squirting it all over the men's hot dogs.*

Britney   Oh, that's lost property.

Lisa   So you've *got* lost property?

Britney   Well, yes and no.

Lisa   Yes and no.

Britney   Well, yes, people are constantly bringing us lost property. But ironically enough, the only lost property they never bring us is the actual Lost Property Office.

Lisa   Yes, but I don't understand. If you've got lots of lost property, surely you're the Lost Property Office anyway?

Britney   No, no, no. That doesn't follow at all.

Lisa   Of course it does – Why not?

As she answers this, a distracted **Britney** *squeezes a constant stream of mustard over* **Ticket**'s *hot dog.*

Britney   Well, you might have a lot of books in your house. But that doesn't make you a library, does it? You might have lots of hot dogs. But that doesn't make you a hot-dog stall, does it?

The flow of mustard ceases.

Everything all right for you?

Ticket   Delicious, thank you.

Britney *returns to the stall.* **Lisa** *follows.*

Britney   Actually, though, between you and me – the funny thing is . . . a couple of weeks back, someone actually *did* hand in a Lost Property Office; just not the one we lost. What are the odds on that? Anyway –

She tips a tray of hot dogs on to the floor.

BIFFER!

Biffer *appears with another load of hot dogs.*

Britney   Get those bloody hot dogs up!

He starts to gather up the hot dogs.

Get the bloody fluff off them!

Lisa   Well, maybe I could visit that one?

As **Biffer** *hands* **Britney** *each hot dog, she throws it down again.*

Britney   What one?

Lisa   The Lost Property Office that someone found but that isn't the Lost Property Office you lost. Can I visit that one?

Everybody stops what they're doing, frozen in fear. **Britney** *doesn't know what to say.*

Britney   I don't know about that. I can't think of any reason why not . . . But I'm sure there must be one.

Pause. **Laughter** *suddenly stands.*

Laughter   I've got a question.

Britney   Yes?

Laughter *brandishes a menu.*

Laughter   It says here – 'Today's Special'.

Britney   Yes?

Laughter   What's so special about it?

A group murmur of appreciation for this question.

Britney   Well . . . it's Biffer's birthday!

Apart from **Biffer** *– who seems unaware of this – they are all delighted by this and offer their congratulations.* **Britney** *leads them in song:*

> Habby burnday to you,
> Habby burnday to you,
> Habby burnday dear Biffer,
> Habby burnday to you.

They applaud. The applause dies down.

Lisa   That's very nice. So do you – ?

Argument   Speech!

They all agree: 'Speech! Speech!'

Britney   Yes, Biffer, give us a speech.

Biffer *climbs up onto a chair and everybody waits for his speech.*

But **Biffer** *says nothing.*

After a time, they all burst into spontaneous applause and appreciation.

Britney   Hot dogs are on the house!

Everyone is appreciative. **Britney***'s tone changes abruptly.*

Britney   BIFFER! HOT DOGS FOR EVERYONE! GET A BLOODY MOVE ON!

Biffer *scurries away for more hot dogs and the men go back to eating and chatting about how wonderful the hot dogs are.*

Lisa   So can I visit the Lost Property now?

Britney (*frustrated*)   It's highly irregular, you know!

Lisa   It'll just be for a minute. I'll give it straight back, I promise.

Britney   You promise?

Lisa   I do, I promise.

Britney *disappears under the counter.*

Lisa *smiles at the diners.*

Britney *resurfaces, now wearing a false beard.*

Laughter *points at* **Britney** *and guffaws loudly. He is silenced by* **Ticket**.

Britney   Lost Property, can I help you?

Pause. **Lisa***'s patience is fraying.*

Lisa   Yes, like I said – I've lost something.

Britney*'s off round the tables again, this time throwing handfuls of fried onions over the ketchup-drenched hot dogs.*

Britney   And what would that be?

Lisa   An hour.

Britney   Can you describe it?

Lisa   Oh – I don't know. How do you describe an hour?

Britney   Well, do you feel heavier since you lost it?

Lisa   Actually, yes, I do.

Britney   So it must be light. If it's light it's daytime. And if it's daytime, it must be big.

Lisa   Why?

Britney   Because the small hours are at night. So it's a big hour, in the day – was it thick or thin?

Lisa   I can't answer that. Hours aren't thick or thin . . .

Britney   All right, then – was it . . . dense? Or was it fine?

Lisa   That's just as stupid, if not more so.

Britney   Not at all. Have you never heard of someone's finest hour?

Lisa   Look – I can't believe there's been that many hours handed in. Can't you just see if my one's there?

Britney   Well, that's very selfish of you! I mean, there's a queue, you know.

The customers murmur their agreement.

Take a ticket and wait your turn. Biffer – where's those bloody hot dogs?!

Lisa *takes a ticket from the ticket roll on the stand.*

Britney   Number seventeen?

Ticket   Oh, that's me!

Argument   Good luck, old boy!

Biffer *rushes out with more hot dogs and collides with* **Ticket***, spilling them all.*

Lisa   Oh dear!

Britney   Biffer, you idiot! Get them picked up!

Britney *and* **Ticket** *kick and beat* **Biffer***, who crawls away.*

Britney *gets a cloth and wipes down* **Ticket***'s jacket.*

Lisa (*to* **Laughter**)   I feel quite sorry for him.

Pause. **Laughter** *guffaws.*

Lisa   What's so funny?

He stops laughing.

Laughter   I don't know – what you said?

Lisa   I just said I felt sorry for him.

He brays with laughter again. **Lisa** *shakes her head.*

Britney   Now – how can I help you?

Ticket   Yes, you see – I was number three earlier.

Britney   Oh yes, I remember.

Ticket   But I lost my ticket.

Britney   I'm sorry, no one's handed in a number-three ticket.

Ticket   So what should I do?

Britney   I'm sure it'll turn up soon.

Ticket   I do hope so.

Ticket *takes another ticket and, munching on a hot dog, returns to his seat.*

Lisa   That's ridiculous.

Argument *stands.*

Argument   I disagree. I think it's eminently reasonable. I'd go so far as to say it was about the most reasonable thing I've either heard or seen ever. Do you concur?

Lisa   No, of course I don't.

Argument   Oh. Right.

Argument *sits down.* **Laughter** *brays out another laugh.*

Lisa   Why do you keep doing that?!

Ticket   He's lost his sense of humour.

Lisa   Oh, I'm sorry. That must be awful for you.

Laughter   Are you being sarcastic?

Lisa   No, not at all.

Laughter   I can't tell, you see. I tend to just laugh and hope it fits. It fits more things than not, I find.

Lisa   How did you lose it?

Ticket   He was the victim of a buse.

Lisa *(not smiling)*   Oh – that's . . . terrible.

Ticket   Isn't it? Especially as the buse has long been considered extinct.

Laughter   In the wild at least.

This irritates **Lisa***. She watches them munch their hot dogs.*

Lisa   There's not much choice of food here, is there?

At the other table, **Argument** *stands, one foot on his chair.*

Argument   I disagree. I've never been anywhere with so much choice. I'm actually dizzy with the amount of choices on offer. I'd go so far as to say there is more choice here than in any other choice-based establishment I've ever visited ever. Would you concur?

Lisa   All they've got is hot dogs!

Argument   Yes. That's true.

He sits down again.

Inhibitions   There's no point arguing with *him*.

Laughter   That's what he's lost.

Lisa   What?

Inhibitions   The argument.

Lisa   Which one?

Argument   Which what?

Lisa   Which argument have you lost?

Argument   Any one you care to mention.

Lisa   But surely that could be fixed?

Argument   How so?

Lisa   Well – you say something and I'll agree with it.

Pause. This hasn't occurred to him.

Ticket   It's worth a try.

Argument   All right – let's give it a try!

There is much murmuring and excitement as **Argument** *approaches one side of the hot-dog stand.* **Britney**, *in turn, takes his seat at the table.* **Lisa** *stands at the opposite end of the stand, and the whole scene begins to resemble a session in Parliament.*

The hubbub dies down for **Argument***'s opening statement.*

Argument   The wild-goose chase – is a cruel and barbaric sport – which should be banned outright!

Noise from all parties, some agreeing, some not.

Lisa   That's not a sport! It's a turn of phrase.

Noise.

Argument   Don't go telling me about wild-goose chases! I'll have you know I used to be a wild-goose-chase saboteur!

Noise.

Lisa   Don't be ridiculous. A wild-goose chase means you're hunting for nothing. How can you sabotage that?

Noise.

Argument   Easily!

Lisa   How?

The noise dies down. Everyone is curious.

Argument   You . . . let loose . . . some geese!

Silence.

Inhibitions *suddenly becomes red-faced and angry, and shouts at the top of his voice:*

Inhibitions   You – Are – Talking – Absolute – *Fucking* – SHIT!

Pause. Everyone's a little taken aback by this.

Argument   Yes. Yes, I am.

He sits down.

Britney   Is everybody all right?!

Everyone nods.

A **Violinist**, *dressed as a giant hot dog (with 'Eat at Britney's' written on her front), appears and begins to play along with the muzak.*

[*Note: it happened to be that in the original production the actress played the violin – it could be another instrument.*]

Ticket   I must say – these hot dogs are absolutely delicious!

Argument   They are – they're excellent!

Laughter   What are they made of?

Britney   Biffer makes them!

Everyone freezes.

We don't know how.

Long pause.

Inhibitions   Well, they are . . . absolutely . . . top-notch.

Everyone agrees and goes back to eating.

Ticket   And so you just put them in a roll . . . ?

Britney   We put them in a roll with onions . . .

Argument   Ah, with onions!

Laughter   Onions, that's what it is!

Ticket   Well, they're really superb.

Britney   Thank you.

Argument   You must give me the recipe.

Britney   Another round?

Argument   Well – I could have another round . . .

Laughter   Yes, why not?

Britney   Biffer – !

Lisa   No, wait a minute, hold on – I'm not all right actually. Could you stop playing that? Could she stop playing that?

The **Violinist** *carries on regardless.*

Lisa   Look – it's nice that you give people food while they're waiting. But maybe if you didn't spend so much time on the food, they wouldn't have to wait so long? I mean, it's just a suggestion.

Britney   Biffer! Where's those bloody hot dogs?!

Lisa   This is so frustrating!

Britney   Ticket number *eighteen*.

Inhibitions   That's me!

Lisa   I don't even believe she's got –

As **Inhibitions** *stands, we realise that he's naked from the waist down.*

Lisa *is shocked.*

Lisa   Oh my God – he's got no pants on!

Inhibitions   I've lost my inhibitions.

Argument *points at* **Inhibition**'s *genitals.*

Argument   Now that *is* funny!

Ticket *nudges* **Laughter**.

Ticket   He's right, it is!

Laughter *guffaws manically.*

Inhibitions *suddenly realises he's naked and drops to the floor in shame, pulling a tablecloth down over him and tipping all the food on to the floor.*

Biffer *comes out with more hot dogs and trips over* **Inhibitions**, *spilling them all.*

Britney   Biffer, you clot!

She sets about **Biffer** *with a kitchen implement. Absolute chaos.*

Lisa *gets up in disgust.*

Lisa   Right, I've had enough of this! I don't even know what I'm doing here! You're all completely mad, the lot of you – and not in a good way!

Lisa *storms off.*

There is laughter and screaming until she has gone and then –

– everybody starts retching and spitting out the hot dogs.

Ticket   I think I'm going to vomit!

Laughter   That was awful!

Argument   Is it true that Biffer makes them?

Britney   I'm afraid so.

A sound of widespread revulsion. **Britney**'s *accent seems to have changed.*

Listen, everybody, I know it wasn't easy. But on behalf of the Dissocian Government, I'd just like to thank you for your contribution to the War Effort. It may seem like a small thing but believe me – anything that helps us stop Lisa finding her hour is extremely valuable. So give yourselves a round of applause . . .

A half-hearted round.

What they don't see is that **Lisa** *has heard it all .*

Britney   As a token of our gratitude, each of you is to be inducted into the Order of the Pulled-Up Socks, for your bravery in the line of –

Lisa   What's going on?

They fall silent.

Argument   Oh dear . . .

Lisa   Anything you can do to stop me finding my hour . . . ?

They all look ashamed.

This was all a fake?

Britney   Lisa –

Lisa   You haven't lost your sense of humour – And you haven't lost the argument – You haven't even lost your inhibitions!

Pause.

Why would you do this? Why don't you want me to find my hour?

Britney   Biffer!

Ticket   Biffer will explain.

Inhibitions   Biffer knows.

Argument   Yes, Biffer.

Biffer *takes a central position. He speaks only in sounds and strange words.* **Lisa** *looks to the others for help in understanding him.*

Biffer *speaks.*

Britney   An hour is a source of tremendous energy. It generates life and it generates death.

Lisa   Yes, I know all that . . .

Biffer *continues.*

Britney   Dissocia is the life your hour generated.

Biffer *continues.*

Inhibitions   Your hour is like the sun to us.

Biffer *continues.*

Laughter   And if you reabsorb your hour −

Biffer *continues.*

Argument   − Dissocia will sweat?

Britney   Die.

Argument   Dissocia will die.

Lisa *absorbs this.*

Lisa   Oh look − you can't put that on me. I mean, I'm sorry I lost my hour, but you can't hold me responsible for what it got up to on its holidays.

Inhibitions   We're only trying to protect you, Lisa.

Lisa   No – you're trying to protect yourselves! And I understand that. I don't want you all to be destroyed. But I've got a life too and it's out of balance. I've got people that I care about – that I love and that love me – and I'm letting them down.

Britney   Nobody loves you more than us, Lisa. Don't you remember?

They gather around her, hemming her in, softly singing:

All
  And now you are our friend we will
  Protect you to the end remember
  No one in the world above will
  Love you like the people of
  This wonderful new world –

Lisa   No! Because if you loved me, you'd help me! I mean, Victor said there'd be people trying to mislead me. But I didn't think it'd be you!

Biffer *starts 'speaking' again.*

Britney   An hour generates life – but it also generates death –

Biffer *continues.*

Inhibitions   And just as we are the life it generated –

Biffer *continues.*

Laughter   The Black Dog King is the death.

All   Queen Sarah, protect us from the Black Dog King.

Biffer *continues.*

Violinist   Your hour contained much good, Lisa . . .

Biffer *continues.*

Argument   But it also contained clogs.

Britney   Evil.

Argument   Evil.

Biffer *continues.*

Laughter   The Destroyer is the embodiment of that evil. We fight him here so that you don't have to.

Ticket   In return you let us live.

Laughter   That is the agreement.

Lisa   I didn't agree to anything. I don't need you to fight my fights for me.

Pause. **Biffer** *walks away.*

Lisa   Where's he going?

Britney   Biffer is disappointed. He's said all he has to say.

Pause.

Lisa   I have to find my hour. I'm sorry but I do.

All   We beg you to reconsider, Lisa.

Britney   The Judas Goat has already made you known to the Destroyer. He has your scent now.

Lisa   But why would he want me? What use am I to him?

Suddenly, there is a rumbling in the distance. They all freeze in fear.

Violinist   INCOMING!

In a panic, they all stuff their gags in their mouths, cover the tops of their heads and assume the safety position.

The wave hits.

But **Lisa** *is still standing, left exposed.*

The others are all in convulsions around her.

Lisa *crouches at first, but slowly stands.*

Eventually, the wave passes. Groaning with discomfort, the others rise.

They see that **Lisa** *has stood there unaffected. A murmur of wonderment ripples through them.*

Inhibitions   She didn't cover her head! Did you see that?

Argument   But she's still alive!

Violinist   How is that possible? How did you withstand the attack?

Lisa   I don't know. It wasn't so bad really.

Britney   It had no effect on you at all?

Lisa   I've got a bit of a headache.

More murmurs of wonderment.

Biffer *has reappeared, bleeding from his ears and eyes.*

Argument   Biffer – Biffer will know!

Violinist   Yes, Biffer –

Inhibitions   Biffer will know!

They all agre that **Biffer** *will know.*

Britney   Biffer, how can this be?

Biffer *'speaks'.*

Britney   There is only one who could withstand an attack unprotected –

Biffer *says something else.*

A pause, and then they all – **Biffer** *included – kneel down before* **Lisa***.*

Britney   All hail, Queen Sarah. You have returned to save us all!

All   ALL HAIL, QUEEN –

Suddenly, **Laughter** *kicks over one of the tables.*

Laughter   Be silent, you fools!

Argument   How dare you, sir! Don't you know –

A collective gasp of shock.

Laughter *and* **Ticket** *have torn off their clothes to reveal that they are wearing dungarees over billowing silk shirts.*

They both have swords and the hats we associate with the musketeers of old France.

Violinist   They're Mungarees!

Laughter   That's right, you cowardly curs! Mungarees! Defenders of the Realm and the Queen's own protectors!

Britney   I thought you'd been disbanded.

Ticket   We had! And we would happily have stayed that way had you not brought ruin on us all!

Lisa   Listen, there must be some mistake. I'm not the Queen of anywhere. I've never even been here before today!

Ticket   There's no mistake, M'Lady. We'll explain later – if we live out the day.

Ticket *takes* **Laughter** *aside.*

Ticket   My friend – we must send for reinforcements!

Laughter   It's too late, my friend. The Queen has been made aware. The Destroyer will be upon us in minutes!

The Dissocians bow down before **Lisa**.

All   Queen Sarah, protect us from the Black Dog King!

Lisa   I can't protect you – tell them!

Ticket   It's true. It is us that must protect our Queen!

Laughter   Quickly, all of you – seize whatever weapons you can!

Inhibitions   We don't stand a chance!

Argument   We'll be slaughtered like buses! (*As previosuly, in 'the victim of a buse'.*)

Laughter   Nonsense! We shall prevail!

Ticket   No, no, don't lie to them. It's true: we will all die in agony and live out the afterlife in excruciating torment!

No one is terribly enthusiastic about this.

But let us not forget why it is that we live!

As the Dissocians listen to this, they hum the tune of 'Dissocia'.

We are strong!

Laughter   And yet we cower in fear!

Ticket   We have one purpose!

Laughter   And yet we fight amongst ourselves!

Ticket   We must remember what we are – citizens of Dissocia, every one! We were born from the very stuff of courage! If we do not fight – we are less than nothing!

Laughter   Now is the time – here and now – that we fulfil our destiny! Now is the time that we fight!

Ticket   For the honour of our Divine Queen Sarah – !

Laughter   And the greater good – of Dissocia!

Ticket   Are you with us?!

Pause. The Dissocians reply as one – 'Yes!'

And then, in the distance, the sound of the Black Dog's approaching army, and their familiar chant:

Army
    Rivers of blood will vein the land!
    Bones will twist inside the hand!
    Children will boil in mothers' wombs!
    Turning on lights will darken rooms!
    And heavy skies will teem with flocks
    Of tiny birds with human cocks!

The Dissocians swallow their fear.

Ticket   Arm yourselves as best you can and prepare for the charge.

The Dissocians gather up implements from the hot-dog stand – a pathetic array of weaponry.

Lisa   No, wait – I don't want you to die for me! Let me face the Black Dog King alone!

Laughter   It may yet come to that, M'Lady. But not until we have spilled Black Dog blood by the pint!

The Mungarees move to the front. The Dissocians form a defence around **Lisa**, *their Queen.*

Together they face the approaching army, the chant growing ever louder.

Laughter   Still – it's good to be back in action, my friend.

Ticket   Indeed. And with our Queen at our side!

Laughter   A Mungaree once more!

Ticket   A Mungaree once more!

They perform the sword salute of the Mungarees.

CHARGE!

And set off towards the enemy, swords aloft.

The Dissocians follow, all of them shouting.

Lisa *watches them disappear into battle.*

The sound is deafening now – the sound of battle – which soon becomes the sound of death, as the Dissocians are slain by the Black Dog army.

Lisa *watches helplessly, in fear and sorrow.*

The sound of the battle finally ceases, and a shadowy figure emerges from the carnage.

Lisa *backs away from him as he walks towards her – backs away until there is nowhere left to go.*

Finally, the Black Dog King steps into the light and **Lisa** *sees his face for the first time.*

It is a face she knows only too well. She shakes her head in horror and disbelief.

Lisa   Oh my God – it's you!

For a moment, the lighting suggests we are back in her flat.

Vince *reaches out – his hands touch her shoulders.*

Blackness.

Act Two

Notes

The whole point of Act Two is that it is the polar opposite of Act One. There should be no overt colour used in set design, costume or lighting. The only sound effects should be the sound of footsteps, which occur only before and after scenes in which Lisa is given medication, and at no other point. The only exception to these two stipulations is in the final scene. Whereas the acting in Act One is stylised, in Act Two the style should be as naturalistic as possible. Accordingly, much of the dialogue in this act – especially in the first scenes – is little more than a sound effect, and the actors should be encouraged to improvise these scenes, using the dialogue as a guideline only, in order to achieve the maximum realism. In the original production, the hospital room was enclosed in a box, the front of which was clear perspex. This necessitated the use of radio mikes for the actors' dialogue. This allowed them to act on a much more intimate scale and was very effective. The set was lit with fluorescent lighting which flickered on and off (in stark contrast to the more fluid style of the first act). This is all very expensive, however, and I know that it will be beyond the reach of most companies. I don't expect fidelity to this design concept; I only mention it in the hope you might honour its spirit as best you can. The stipulations of no colour/no sound will mean that the hospital room will not be an accurate representation of modern psychiatric centres, which tend to be quite colourful places. It is important to me, however, that this play does not seem biased against the notion of psychiatric treatment; on some level, such treatment is always about the suppression of individuality which already loads the dramatic dice somewhat. In light of this, I would ask directors/designers to be careful not to tip the dice even further. For example, it's important that the room has a window: to omit a window would hint at an unacceptably inhumane environment. Similarly, the actors should endow the nurses, staff and relatives with a basic warmth, despite actions that may read as cold and impersonal. The play will be more interesting for it.

One

Lights up.

A room in a psychiatric hospital.

Lisa *lies, asleep, in a hospital bed.*

The sound of footsteps approaching.

The door opens.

Nurse 1 *enters. Gently, she nudges* **Lisa** *awake. She helps* **Lisa***, who is very drowsy, into a sitting position.*

She puts two pills in the palm of **Lisa***'s hand and helps them to her mouth.*

She pours a glass of water and holds it to **Lisa***'s mouth.*

Lisa *manages to swallow the pills.* **Nurse 1** *makes sure of this.*

Lisa *lies down again, goes back to sleep.*

Nurse 1 *covers her shoulder with the sheet, then leaves.*

The sound of her footsteps as she walks away, down the corridor.

Lights down.

Two

Lights up.

Lisa *is asleep.*

The sound of footsteps approaching.

Nurse 2 *enters.*

Gently, he nudges **Lisa** *awake.*

Nurse 2 *helps her into a sitting position, gives her some pills and some water to wash them down with.*

Lisa *lies down again, goes back to sleep.*

Nurse 2 *covers her shoulder with the sheet, then leaves.*

The sound of his footsteps as he walks away.

Lights down.

Three

Lisa *is slumped in bed, awake.*

Decisively, she gets up, gathers her belongings and leaves the room.

Pause.

The sound of muffled voices.

She re-enters, ushered in by **Nurse 3**.

Lisa   I just want to use the phone –

Nurse 3   That's fine, you can use the phone.

Lisa   I've got a right to use the phone.

Nurse 3   Right, well, you leave your stuff here and I'll take you to the phone, fair enough?

Pause. Reluctantly, **Lisa** *hands over her armful of belongings.*

Lisa   And I want to have a cigarette.

Nurse 3   Right, well, after we've gone to the phone, I'll take you to the smoking room and you can have a cigarette. Come on.

Pause.

Lisa   Look, I don't need this, I'm fine now. I'd be better off at home –

Nurse 3   You'll be home soon enough.

Lisa   But it's not doing me any good here, I'd feel much better at home, you know – with all my things around me . . .

Nurse 3   Why don't you get back into bed?

Lisa   I don't want to go back to bed! I'm fine now, I'm ready, I'll take my medication, I swear – !

Nurse 3   Come on, back to bed.

Reluctantly, **Lisa** *gets back in.* **Nurse 3** *puts her belongings back where they came from.*

Nurse 3   That's a girl. Listen – as soon as you're better, you'll be turfed out, believe me. We need the beds.

Lisa *sulks.*

Nurse 3   Now don't be creeping around cos I'll be watching.

Nurse 3 *exits.*

Lisa *fumes for a while, then tears get the better of her.*

She puts the pillow over her head.

Lights down.

Four

Lights up.

Lisa *is asleep. The pillow is on the floor.*

The sound of footsteps.

Nurse 1 *enters and jostles her awake.*

She helps **Lisa** *into a sitting position and administers medication.*

Lisa *goes back to sleep.*

Lights down.

Five

Lights up.

The sound of footsteps.

Lisa *lies in bed, slumped but awake. She looks hostile.*

Nurse 2 *enters.*

Nurse 2   Hi there.

*He empties some pills into **Lisa**'s hand and pours her a glass of water.*

Here we go.

Resentfully, she takes the pills.

Nurse 2 *exits.*

Lisa *puts her Walkman on.*

She listens.

The tinny sound of music, which we might just be able to recognise as the punky music from the flying car sequence in Act One.

She nods her head.

Lights down.

Six

*The sound of **Lisa** singing raucously.*

Lights up.

Lisa *is dancing manically around the room, on the bed, everywhere, Walkman in her hand.*

Nurse 1 *enters accompanied by **Nurse 3**, and attempts to take the Walkman away from **Lisa**, who resists.*

Lisa   No!

Nurse 3 *restrains her, with as little contact as possible, and manages to get the Walkman. She wraps the headphone cable around it.*

Lisa   What are you doing?

Nurse 1   You're supposed to be resting, Lisa.

Lisa   You can't take that, it's mine!

Nurse 1   You can have it back when you've calmed down.

Lisa   Right, I'm calm, I'm totally calm, see? I was just dancing, but now I'm totally calm, so you can give it back to me.

Nurse 1   Later.

Lisa   No, listen, you don't understand – I need it, I really need it –

Nurse 1   You'll get it back when you've calmed down.

Lisa   Give it back to me, you fucking cow!

Nurse 1 *exits, followed by* **Nurse 3**.

Lisa   I was just dancing! What the fuck is wrong with dancing?!

Pause.

Like a petulant child, **Lisa** *continues to dance and sing, but soon she is tired out, and she crumples to the floor, in tears.*

Lights down.

Seven

Lights up.

Lisa *is asleep on the floor, where she fell.*

The sound of footsteps.

Nurse 3 *enters, helps her up.*

Nurse 3   Oh dear, come on – up we get.

Nurse 3 *helps a compliant* **Lisa** *up into the bed.*

Lisa *adopts a sleeping position immediately, but* **Nurse 3** *interrupts her, sitting her up and giving* **Lisa** *her medication, which she takes obediently.*

Lisa *lies down again.*

Nurse 3 *exits.*

The sound of footsteps as he walks away.

Lights down.

Eight

Lights up.

Lisa *sits in bed, waiting.*

The door opens and a doctor enters.

Dr Clark   Lisa? I'm Dr Clark.

*She shakes **Dr Clark**'s hand.*

Lisa   I've actually got a doctor.

Dr Clark   Dr Spence, I know. But you'll be seeing me for a while if that's all right?

Pause.

He sits down and opens her notes.

So – you've been having a bit of a time, haven't you?

Pause.

Lights down.

Nine

Lights up.

Lisa *is in bed, reading – but the movement of her feet beneath the sheets betrays her lack of concentration. She has to keep turning the page back and starting again.*

Nurse 2 *enters.*

Nurse 2   Hello again.

He empties the pills into **Lisa***'s hand and pours her a glass of water.*

Lisa *stares at them.*

Lisa   Are these the same ones as before?

Nurse 2   Before when?

Lisa   It's just I asked Dr Clark about some other pills. He said he'd see if there was anything less heavy.

Pause.

Nurse 2   These are what it says on your sheet.

Lisa   Yes, but he said he'd try find something lighter because these ones make me feel really dopey?

Nurse 2 (*nods*)   Right . . .

Pause.

But these are what it says on the sheet.

Pause.

Lisa *takes them.*

Nurse 2 *points at* **Lisa***'s book.*

Nurse 2   What's that like?

Lisa   I don't know. I can't focus on it, on the words.

Nurse 2   Oh, right . . .

Lisa   That's another thing about them.

Nurse 2   Yeah – oh well; heard it's not that good anyway. Just wait for the film, maybe. Bye then.

Nurse 2 *exits.*

It's an insensitive comment but, for the first time in this act, **Lisa** *smiles.*

Lights down.

Ten

Lisa *is asleep.*

The door of **Lisa***'s room has a window in it, so nurses can look in.*

The curtain pulls back and **Nurse 1** *does exactly this.*

All is well. **Nurse 1** *continues with her rounds, leaving the curtain drawn.*

Eleven

Lisa*'s sister,* **Dot***, sits in the chair by her bed.*

She is mending a child's ballet shoe.

Dot   The thing is, in the end of the day, it's just selfishness, Lisa, it really is. I know that sounds harsh, but it is. If you saw how worried she was . . .

Lisa *is slumped in bed, feeling a bit nauseous.*

Dot   You know what happened to Auntie Liz. You want to end up like that? How d'you think that'd make Mum feel? How do you think it'd make me feel? And all because you can't manage to take a few pills twice a day.

Pause.

I mean, do you want everyone to think you're some sort of nut-case? I know you're not, but that's what people think and you can't blame them.

Pause.

I mean, I can help you out now and then, but I've got a mortgage to pay; I don't make the payments, I'm out on the street, and who's going to take me in? And meanwhile, you're out there merrily buying shoes and handbags and things you'll never use –

Pause.

I mean, I've tried being nice, I've tried everything. But now you're just going to have to take the consequences. We can't all be floating around with our heads in the clouds, playing the guitar and being 'artistic'. The sooner you get that through your head, the better. This is the real world.

Pause.

Dot A few pills, twice a day, that's all you've got to manage. I take four myself and they're only vitamins – I don't end up scribbling on the walls if I miss a day, but I still manage to take them. And if you don't care enough about yourself, then at least do it for Mum and for Mark and for me. I mean how do you think I feel, knowing everyone thinks my sister's a loony?

Lisa Dot, I'm sorry but I'm really feeling sick . . .

Dot You haven't heard a thing I've said, have you?

Lisa No, I have, I just – need to rest now.

Huffily, **Dot** *puts the shoes in her handbag and gets up.*

Dot I know how you feel.

She exits.

Lights down.

Twelve

Lights up.

Lisa *looks down at the Walkman in her hand.*

She puts the headphones on, presses play.

The same tinny music.

But this time, there is no movement.

She just listens.

Lights down.

Thirteen

Lights up.

Lisa *sits up in bed, reading.*

She seems more concentrated now.

The door opens and a doctor comes in, holding **Lisa**'s *notes.*

Dr Faraday   Sorry about the wait – Lisa, is it?

She sits up. He offers his hand, which she shakes.

Dr Faraday   Dr Faraday. But call me Peter.

Pause.

Lisa   What happened to Dr Clark?

Lights snap out.

Fourteen

Lights up.

Lisa *is reading. She's almost finished her book.*

The sound of footsteps approaching.

She marks her place in the book, puts it down on the bedside cabinet.

She pours herself some water.

Nurse 1 *enters.*

Nurse 1   Hi there.

Lisa   Hello.

Nurse 1 *hands the pill container to* **Lisa**, *then goes to draw the curtains.*

Lisa *takes her pills.*

Nurse 1   Lovely weather out there.

Lisa   Yes, I was out for a while.

Nurse 1   Indian summer.

Lisa   Yeah. Probably be pissing down by the weekend.

Nurse 1   Well – as long as it doesn't rain on Thursday.

Lisa   What's happening Thursday?

Nurse 1   Friend of mine's getting married.

Lisa   Oh, that's nice.

Nurse 1   Yes, well – good excuse for a party, isn't it?

Lisa   Yeah. Well – don't get *too* drunk.

Nurse 1   I'll try. All right then –

Lisa   See you then.

Nurse 1 *exits.*

Lisa *looks at the sunlight pouring through the window.*

She sighs.

Lights down.

Fifteen

Lights up.

Lisa *is sitting, fully upright, in bed.*

She looks at herself in a compact mirror, adjusts her hair, puts the mirror away.

She takes a deep breath.

Vince *enters. He's carrying a plastic bag full of things.*

He hugs her, but there's a lack of affection in it.

He sits in the chair.

Vince   How are you?

Lisa   Fine. Good, actually.

Vince   Good.

Pause.

Lisa   How's work?

Vince   Oh, you know – hectic. Same as ever.

Pause.

I'm sorry I couldn't get away –

Lisa   It's fine.

Pause.

Vince   I mean, I probably could've but –

Lisa   Honestly, it's fine. I don't want you to mess up your work because of me. I feel bad enough as it is.

Pause.

Vince   You don't have to feel bad.

Pause.

But you're feeling better now?

Lisa   Much.

Vince   Good.

Pause.

Lisa   Roll on Sunday is all.

He nods, smiling humourlessly. Pause.

Simultaneously:

Vince   Lisa, I –

Lisa   Vince, I –

They laugh.

Lisa   You first.

Vince   No – you.

Pause.

Lisa   I just want to say that I'm sorry. I'm sorry for all the trouble I cause everyone. I don't mean to. I just . . .

He nods. Pause.

Vince   But it's difficult, you know – ?

Lisa (*nods*)   I know.

Vince   I mean, you say you don't mean to. But you know what happens when you come off the medication. This happens. Sooner or later you end up here.

Lisa (*nods*)   I know.

Vince   Yeah, but it's not *enough* to say that you know! I mean, why – ?

Pause.

I thought you wanted to get better.

Lisa   I *do* want to get better.

Vince   Well, yes, you say that but then you don't take your *medication* –

Lisa *sighs heavily.*

Vince   Yeah, well, you can fucking sigh, but what can I do? All I can do is nag you to take the fucking pills and then you resent me for nagging you, I just –

Pause.

I don't know if I can do this any more, I really don't –

Lisa   Vince – I'm really going to try –

Vince   You say that / *every* time!

Lisa   I know! I know I do, but you don't understand –

Vince   That's not my fault! It's not my fault that I don't understand!

Lisa   I'm not saying / it is –

Vince   I mean, I've got a message from you on my phone. Do you want to hear it?

He takes out his mobile phone and pushes it at her.

She doesn't want to hear.

Because it's just nonsense. You're just, you're saying – nonsense!

Pause.

Lisa   So what are you saying? You want to leave me?

Vince   *Leave* you . . .

Lisa   Split up with me.

Long pause.

You know what it is: it's like the Sirens.

Pause.

Vince   The Sirens?

Lisa   You know. They sit on the rocks and they sing to the sailors. And what they sing is so lovely it's like . . . they're hypnotised. They know if they sail to them their ship's going to get all smashed up. But they think it's worth it, you know – for the song.

Long pause.

Vince   I should go.

Pause. She nods.

Got to finish this proposal. Here's your stuff.

He hands her the plastic bag. She nods her thanks.

Pause.

Lisa   Will you come for me on Sunday?

Pause.

Or should I make other plans?

Pause.

Vince   That thing you said. About the Sirens.

Pause.

I understand that. That's how it is for me, with you.

Pause.

I'll see you Sunday.

He exits.

Pause.

Lisa *lifts things out of the plastic bag: a jumper, another book, some bills from home.*

Then she sees something at the bottom of the bag.

She smiles affectionately.

Lights down.

Sixteen

Night. **Lisa** *is asleep. She looks at peace. In her arms she holds a small polar bear.*

We hear music at last.

Coloured lights play on her face, swirling around her head.

Dissocia still exists, caged within her head.

There is little doubt that she will return to her kingdom.

The music ends.

Lights down.

End.

Realism

Notes

While the dialogue in this play is largely my own, the material herein was hugely influenced by the suggestions, criticisms and improvisations of the actors and creative team, whose names are listed in the text.

As ever, what follows is a record of a show that was presented in 2006. Elements of the sound or production design may be described, but should only be taken into account; they represent no stipulation on my part (except where indicated).

The play contains references to topical events, localised matters and personal issues that may limit its relevance in other territories or times. Where possible, I have attempted to explain the dramatic relevance of these moments so that the imaginative translator may find a way to adapt them.

Though *Realism* is divided into acts, it should be presented without an interval.

Please note that though there are several phone conversations during the play, at no point should a phone ever be present (or represented) onstage.

THE SET

In the original production, the stage was raked from front to back with a slight imbalance upstage left.

All the elements of a normal home were present. From front of stage to back: a sofa, a fridge with work surface, a washing machine, a toilet, a bed, a dining table and chairs, an armchair, etc. Various practical lights (both standing and hanging) were also arranged around the set.

However, the stage itself was covered with several tons of off-white sand. All of the aforementioned furniture was cut off to varying degrees (and at varying angles) so as to appear 'sunk' into this sand. The television was placed at the very front of the stage, seeming almost completely submerged, allowing only enough space to use it as a lighting source for the sofa.

The walls on all three sides consisted of large pillars, grey and textured, which hinted at concrete. Actors entered and exited between them.

PRE-SHOW

As the audience arrived, we played a medley of UK traditional tunes which was famously (until 2006) used as the opening music for BBC Radio 4. It not only set the play's beginning firmly in the morning; it also inspired a spirit of joviality, which I would recommend – as *Realism* is, to all intents and purposes, a comedy. If you have any kind of equivalent – a light tune that your audience finds synonymous with morning – I would respectfully suggest that you consider its use.

'Breakdowns' are presented in square brackets at the scene beginnings. These describe what is actually occurring in the play's 'real' time-line. I wrote them for my own benefit and present them for your interest only. You may prefer not to read them, and experience the show in the same vague sense of confusion that the audience did.

Characters

Stuart
Paul
Mother
Father
Mullet
Angie
Presenter
Pundit
Right-Wing Politician
Left-Wing Politician
Independent Politician
Audience Member
Laura
Minstrel 1
Minstrel 2
Minstrel 3
Simon
Cat
Bystanders

Act One: Morning

One

[*In which . . .* **Stuart** *gets a phone call from his friend* **Paul**. **Paul** *wants him to come and play football.* **Stuart** *declines the offer. He puts out some food for the cat. He remembers a dream he had the previous night. He goes back to bed.*]

Stuart *sits on the couch, in his bedclothes. He has one hand down his pants, absent-mindedly squeezing himself – it is not a sexual gesture. He looks very tired.*

Paul, *wearing a suit, is looking in the fridge.*

Paul Did I wake you?

Stuart No, not really.

Paul Not really?

Stuart I was awake.

Paul Were you still in bed?

Stuart *smells his fingers.*

Stuart Yeah, well, it's Saturday morning so . . .

Paul So I woke you up. I'm sorry.

Pause.

Stuart What's going on?

Paul Were you out last night?

Stuart For a while.

He tries to look at a birthmark on his shoulder. It's itching.

Paul D'you get pissed?

Stuart A bit.

Paul A bit?

Stuart   Paul – I've not even had a cup of tea –

Paul   I was just wondering what you're up to. You playing fives later?

He starts dribbling a football back and forward.

Stuart   I don't know. I don't think so.

Paul   You've got to.

Stuart   Why have I got to?

Paul   We're already a man down.

Stuart   I don't think I can.

Paul   Why not?

Stuart   I just – I don't really feel like it.

Pause.

Paul   What do you feel like, then?

Stuart   What?

Paul   What do you feel like doing?

Stuart   Not much.

Paul   Aw, come on – come and play football. We'll have a few pints.

*For the first time we see **Paul** from the front. His shirt is half open and his suit jacket has vomit down it.*

Stuart   I really don't feel like it.

Paul   So what are you going to do? Just mope about your flat all day?

Stuart   I've got stuff to do.

Paul   Like what?

Stuart   Just boring things.

Paul   Like what?

Stuart   For fuck's sake . . .

Paul   I'm just asking.

Stuart   Like washing, cleaning up – domestic shit.

Paul   You can do that tomorrow.

Stuart   I can't.

Paul   Why not?

Stuart   Cos I just – I haven't got any clean clothes . . . I just need to get myself together.

Paul *crosses to the couch and sits beside* **Stuart***.*

Paul   I could come over after. Get a few cans in. Get a DVD out.

He instantly falls asleep. During the next exchange, he nods in and out of consciousness.

Stuart   Paul, I really – I just want to do nothing.

Paul   You want to do nothing?

Stuart   Yeah, I just –

Paul   We don't have to do anything. We can just kiss and cuddle a bit; there's no pressure.

Stuart   That's tempting.

Pause.

No, really, I just – I said to myself I was just going to do nothing today. It's been a fucking hellish week at work and I'm just knackered; just want to chill out.

Paul   What good – do you?

Stuart   Eh?

Paul   That going to – ?

Pause. Annoyed, **Stuart** *stands.*

Paul   Damned reception.

Stuart   Fucking things.

Paul   I said what good's it going to do you, moping about your flat all day?

Stuart   I'm not going to be moping.

Paul   You are – you're going to mope.

Stuart   I'm not going to mope.

Paul   Mope, mope, mope; that'll be you.

Stuart   Right, well, so if I want to mope I can fucking mope, can't I? I mean, I'm not planning on moping but I reserve the right to mope in my own fucking house.

Paul   All right, all right; calm down, calm down. I just don't want you getting all depressed.

Stuart   I'm not, I'm fine.

Paul   All right.

Stuart   Just want to spend a bit of time on my own.

Paul   Fair enough.

He staggers to his feet.

Will I give you – tomorrow?

Stuart   Will you give me tomorrow?

Paul (*louder*)   Will I give you a *shout* tomorrow?

Stuart   Yeah, give me a shout tomorrow.

Paul   If you change your mind –

Stuart   I'll give you a bell.

Paul   Give us a bell. We'll be in the Duck's Arse from about five.

Stuart   All right, cheers.

Paul *exits.*

Pause. **Stuart** *yawns.*

Stuart *goes to the fridge, opens it. He takes out a tin of cat food and prises back the lid. He fills a bowl with food. Some of it drops onto the floor. At the top of his voice he shouts:*

Here, kitty kitty kitty kitty!

He considers staying awake, but then walks back towards his bedroom.

On the way, his **Mother** *appears. He stops.*

Mother   Have you seen the sky?

Stuart   What do you mean?

Mother   It's full of bombers.

Stuart   Where from?

Mother   Israel? [*At the time of writing, in 2006, Israel had invaded Lebanon. Substitute a more topical/timeless reference if necessary.*]

Pause. **Stuart** *continues on his way.*

Mother *takes a seat at the dining table.*

Stuart *climbs back into bed.*

Lights fade. Music – during which **Father** *enters, carrying a morning paper. He takes a seat at the dining table, handing part of the paper to* **Mother**. *They read.*

Two

[**Stuart** *gets up again. He remembers another fragment of a dream. He makes himself a cup of tea, and gets a mild electric shock from the toaster. Feeling bad about himself, he attempts to exercise but ends up pretending to be a rabbit. He remembers a friend chasing him with a shit-covered stick. The same friend got him to taste a crayon, which was horrible. He watches a news report about the Middle East crisis.*]

Stuart *wakes up with cramp. He hits the side of his leg. The pain passes. Pause.*

Paul *enters behind* **Stuart**, *carrying a huge carrot.* **Stuart** *doesn't see him.*

Paul   Stuart.

Stuart   What?

Paul   That fucking squirrel's back.

Stuart   What does he want?

Paul   He wants his guts back in.

Stuart   That'll cost a fortune.

Paul   Yeah, but Angie'll pay for it. She's on her way out.

Paul *sits in the armchair.*

Stuart *gets up and collects a cup from the cupboard.*

Father   Stuart, don't bother me.

On his way to the fridge, **Stuart** *looks inside the cup, checking that it's clean. He turns on the electric kettle.*

Mother   Can you see it? There – a castle, look. The tea leaves make a turret, and the tea's like a moat at the bottom.

Stuart   What's a moat?

Mother   It's the water round a castle, to keep the folk from getting in.

Simultaneously, **Mother** *and* **Stuart** *sing a fairly buoyant, very British wartime song – the sort of song a mother used to sing:*

   I like a nice cup of tea in the morning,
   I like a nice cup of tea with my tea . . .

But **Mother***'s voice fades away, leaving* **Stuart** *groping for the lyrics. A sound arrives, punching into him the realisation of her absence.* **Mullet** *takes up the tune, humming to himself.*

Stuart *takes a moment to recover, then puts the cup down. He looks at the jars in front of him.*

Stuart   Coffee – tea? Tea – coffee?

Optionally, the sound of monkeys (as in the famous series of British TV tea commercials, featuring chimpanzees).

Stuart *opens a box of tea bags. He drops a tea bag into the cup.*

He opens the fridge.

He takes out a packet of bread. He snaps off two pieces and pushes them into the toaster. He takes some milk out of the fridge. He smells the milk.

The sound of children playing

The sound of the water boiling in the kettle becomes the sound of horses galloping. It reaches a crescendo . . . then stops.

He pours the hot water into the mug.

Smoke is beginning to rise from the toaster. The bread is trapped in there.

Mullet (*in an annoying sing-song*)   Stewpot! Stewpot! Stewpot! [*This is what many children called Stuart were nicknamed in the seventies.*]

Stuart *tries to get the toaster to eject the toast but it isn't working. He's beginning to panic.*

Mullet *appears behind the couch. He looks like a child from the seventies. He is hyperactive and extremely irritating.*

Mullet   Stewpot! Stewpot! Stewpot!

Stuart   For fuck's sake, what?!

Mullet   The toast's burning!

Stuart   I know! I can't get it out.

Mullet   Use a knife!

Stuart   I'll get electrocuted.

Mullet   You won't.

Panicked, **Stuart** *runs to the cutlery drawer and runs back to the toaster.*

He plunges the knife into the toaster and is immediately thrown on to his back by the resulting shock. **Mullet** *finds this hilarious.*

Mullet (*gleeful*)   You fucking knob!

Angrily, **Stuart** *smacks the toaster off the surface.*

Mullet   That was a fucking beauty!

Stuart   My heart's going like the clappers!

Pause.

Fucking hell.

He picks up the toaster and the burnt toast. He takes a knife to the toast and starts to scrape off the burnt bits.

Angie *appears behind him, wearing a dressing gown. She stops, annoyed.*

Angie   Why do you do that?

Stuart   What?

Angie   Scrape the fucking toast into the sink?

Stuart   I don't like burnt toast.

Angie   So scrape it into the fucking bin! It just clogs the sink up. And then you smear it on the side of the Flora [*a type of margarine*]. You're a dirty bastard.

She continues across the stage.

Stuart   I thought you were going to call me?

She exits.

Pause. **Stuart** *throws the toast into the pedal bin.*

He walks over to the sofa, sits down.

Stuart   I've broke out in a sweat from that shock.

Mullet   That was a beauty. You went fucking flying!

Stuart *tries to look at his mole.*

Mullet   What's wrong?

Stuart   That birthmark's itching.

Mullet   Let's see.

He takes a look at it.

I'm not joking, man; that's cancer.

Stuart   It's not cancer. I'm too young to have cancer.

Mullet   You're joking, aren't you? Fucking Kylie's got cancer – look how young she is! If someone with all that money and an arse like that can get cancer, you think you can't? What else is wrong with you?

Stuart   My left eye's still funny.

Mullet   That's diabetes.

Stuart   It's not diabetes!

He goes to the mirror, distressed. Behind him, **Mullet** *makes faces and rude signs.*

Mullet   Why not? Your uncle had it.

Stuart   Doesn't mean I've got it.

Mullet   So why are you thirsty all the time?

Stuart   Am I thirsty all the time?

He thinks about it.

I'm thirsty a lot of the time. And I keep getting cramp. Is that diabetes?

Mullet (*mimics*)   'Is that diabetes?' You're such a fucking jessie.

Stuart   Fuck you.

Mullet   What's happened to you, man? You were going to be a choo-choo driver. You were going to be an astronaut. What's happened to that guy? What's happened to the guy who was going to build a rocket and fly to fucking Mars? I mean, look at yourself. What do you see?

Pause.

Stuart   A fat fucking shite.

Mullet   A fat fucking shite. And how do you feel?

Stuart   Like shite.

Mullet   Like shite. And what are you going to do about it?

Stuart   Fuck all.

Mullet   You're going to do fuck all. You could have gone out to play footie but you're going to sit around the house all day moping and why? Because of a girl! Because you're waiting for a girl to call you!

Stuart   I can't help it. I love her.

Mullet (*mimics*)   'I loooove her'! So why did you dump her then?

Stuart   I didn't.

Mullet   You did. You dumped her because she had horrible, wobbly thighs and a wonky fucking nose.

Stuart   Shut your stupid face.

Mullet   It's true.

Stuart   It's not!

Pause.

Mullet   Hey, Stu – do that thing with your pants!

Pause. **Stuart** *pulls his pants up over his belly. Cranking one arm, he lets his belly extend to its full size, as if pumping it up. Then he removes an imaginary cork from his belly and lets it deflate.*

Mullet   *That* – is fucking *genius*.

Stuart   I'm a fat sack of shit.

Mullet   So what? So's Tony Soprano and he gets shags. And you know why? Because only poofs care what they look like. And women know that.

Stuart *gets on to the floor.*

Mullet   What are you doing? Are you going to do press-ups? Only wanks do press-ups.

Stuart *starts doing press-ups.*

Stuart   I'm not listening to you.

Mullet *gets down beside him and moves and talks in rhythm with* **Stuart***'s increasingly laboured exercises.*

Mullet   Good. So you won't hear me say how *boring* they are, and what a *poof* you are, and how *boring* they are, and what a *wank* you are, and how boring they are, and how *fat* you are, and what a *weakling* you are –

Stuart *gives up, knackered and exasperated, and strangely amused.*

Mullet   How many was that?

Stuart   Four. (*Or however many he managed.*)

Mullet *derides him.*

Mullet   Four! You only managed four?!

Stuart   I'm going to build them up over time.

He stands up and starts to jump up and down, on the spot.

Mullet   Look at you now! You look like a fucking rabbit!

Stuart   Do I?

Mullet (*excited*)   Do this – Stu – do this.

Hopping alongside **Stuart**, **Mullet** *makes paws with his hands and sticks his teeth out.*

Mullet   Like a rabbit!

Stuart *does it.*

Mullet   Are you hungry, rabbit?

Stuart *nods.*

Mullet   You want some carrots?

He nods.

Say, 'I want some carrots, Mr Farmer.'

Stuart   'I want some carrots, Mr Farmer.'

Mullet *offers his crayons.*

Mullet   Right – Imagine these are carrots! Come and get the carrots.

Stuart *follows after* **Mullet**.

Mullet   No, but you have to hop.

Stuart *hops after him.*

Mullet   That's it – come and get the carrots, Thumper!

Stuart *reaches him but* **Mullet** *suddenly produces a stick.*

Stuart   What's that?

Mullet   It's a stick!

Stuart   What's on the end of it?

Mullet   Keich! [*Scottish slang for shit.*]

Stuart   Fuck off – is it?

Mullet   Smell it.

Tentatively **Stuart** *does – he gags.*

Stuart   Aw, fuck off!

Grinning, **Mullet** *chases after him.*

Stuart   Fuck off! Fuck off, ya dirty bastard!

They run around laughing, and occasionally gagging.

Mullet *whoops like a Red Indian and suddenly lots of others appear, as if in a playground. He chases them all around and for a moment the stage is full of noise and activity. One by one they claim sanctuary by the walls. Finally, out of breath,* **Stuart** *is cornered.*

Stuart   Put that down.

Mullet   Why?

Stuart   (*gags*) Just put it down. I'm telling you.

Mullet   Telling me what?

Stuart   Telling you to put it down.

Mullet *thrusts at him.*

Stuart   You better fucking not – I'm telling you.

Mullet   You want the carrots? Are you going to hop to the carrots?

Stuart   I'll hop to the carrots if you put it down.

Pause. **Mullet** *puts it down.*

Stuart *advances a little.* **Mullet** *quickly picks it up and thrusts it at him.*

Stuart   Put the fucking thing down!

Mullet   All right, all right – I'm putting it down.

He puts it down, then throws the orange crayons.

Hop to the carrots, rabbit.

Stuart *hops over to the carrots.*

Mullet   Eat one.

Pause. **Stuart** *eats the end of one. He spits it out in disgust.*

Stuart   That's fucking awful!

The game's over – **Stuart** *sits on the couch.*

Mullet   Stewpot! Stuart! Stuart.

Stuart *ignores him.*

He picks up his tea and sips it. He turns the TV on – its light plays on his face.

Dejected, **Mullet** *gathers up his things and leaves, dragging his stick behind him.*

The sounds of war.

Behind him, people run screaming as if under heavy fire, taking shelter behind the appliances.

Oblivious to them, **Stuart** *crosses to the fridge and fixes himself a bowl of cereal.*

He arrives back at the couch as the same time as the others, who assemble themselves around him.

Three

[**Stuart** *gets annoyed by a radio discussion show in which the guests all seem to be in favour of the smoking ban (introduced in Scotland in 2006). a pirate radio station interferes with the reception. He imagines himself a member of the panel. He considers how to get* **Angie** *to call him.*]

Pundit   The simple fact is that this is a blight on our society and a drain on the already stretched resources of the Health Service; and if the pitiful souls that participate in it do not have either the ability or the moral fibre to control themselves, then it's actually our societal *duty* to make sure they can do as little harm to others as possible.

Applause.

Presenter   Remind me what your party's position on the ban is, Right-Wing Politician McDonald?

Right-Wing Politician   My party's position –

Left-Wing Politician   I don't think the Conservatives have a position.

A spattering of laughter and applause from the audience. **Stuart**, *sandwiched between them, continues to eat his breakfast.*

Right-Wing Politician   No, actually, our position is that we're broadly in favour of the ban –

Left-Wing Politician   Broadly.

Right-Wing Politician   But that we argued for certain exemptions, such as private clubs.

Left-Wing Politician   Conservative clubs by any chance?

Some laughter.

Presenter   And what's your personal view?

Right-Wing Politician   My personal view –

Presenter   Given that the question was whether the current smoking ban is an infringement of civil liberties.

Right-Wing Politician   Right, well – it obviously is an infringement on the civil liberties of smokers –

The sound of a pirate radio station cuts in – booming dance music.

Stuart   Oh fuck –

In unison, the panel members all get up and crab-walk across the stage, stopping here and there, until, finally, the reception returns.

Right-Wing Politician   But is their right to smoke more important than the rights of those who don't?

And then cautiously – so as not to lose reception – they back on to the couch, as one.

Independent Politician   So it's a question of whose rights are more important?

Right-Wing Politician   Exactly.

Independent Politician   Which is exactly the Labour Party's position.

Right-Wing Politician   I was asked what *my* opinion was.

Pundit   A more important question is why should the general public have to pay billions of pounds a year to help cure these wretched individuals of their self-inflicted ailments?

Applause.

Stuart   I'm sorry but the hypocrisy here is absolutely stunning. I mean, they've banned smoking at bus stops!

Pundit   I should think so.

Stuart   All right, well, tell me this: if cigarettes are *so toxic* that it's dangerous even to *stand near a smoker at a bus-stop* . . . why are we selling them at all? Why not ban them altogether?

Presenter   That's a good point, isn't it, Jan Pearson? Why not ban them altogether?

Left-Wing Politician   Well, that really *would* be an infringement on civil liberties –

Stuart   Oh, what bollocks! If you were concerned about civil
liberties you wouldn't have banned the right to demonstrate
outside Parliament!

A solitary cheer from the audience.

Thank you. I mean, let's say we suddenly found out that
fucking – Pot Noodle – was so horrendously poisonous – that
just being in the same *building* as someone eating it was
potentially fatal: are you saying we'd keep it on the shelves?

Left-Wing Politician   A slightly different thing.

Stuart   Yes, it is, and we all know why; because the
government isn't making £3.50 worth of taxes on every Pot
Noodle sold!

*Some applause. He gets up and crosses to the fridge to get more milk for
his cereal.*

All I'm saying is, make your minds up: if smoking's legal, then
let people do it. Let the pubs and the restaurants and the
workplaces decide whether they allow it or not. But if it's as
dangerous as you say it is – and you're genuinely concerned
about the health of the nation – then have the guts to ban it
outright . . .

Applause. Warming to his theme (and still eating his cereal):

. . . but you won't, will you? because you don't want everyone
to suddenly stop smoking. Because if everyone stopped
smoking, they'd have to raise income tax by about two pence
in the pound; and the people that'd shout loudest about it are
the same wankers that are shouting about having to pay
smokers' health bills.

Hitting his stride now, he adopts the manner of a lawyer.

You see, what we have in the smoking ban is an unholy
alliance between –

*He stands in the spilled cat food. Disgusted, he scrapes it off his bare foot
while continuing:*

What we have in the smoking ban is an unholy alliance
between the hypocritical and the sanctimonious. On the one
hand, we've got a government who want the nation to get
healthier, but not so suddenly that it jeopardises their chances
of re-election. And on the other hand, we've got a society – a
post-Thatcherite society – that is so fractured and dysfunctional
that the only way a semblance of unity can be preserved is to
feed it a constant stream of state-approved scapegoats for us to
mutually fear or disdain.

Now to the audience:

In summing up, I can put it no better than the famous poem
written by some Jewish guy or possibly a German:

> When they came for the gays
> I did not speak out
> Because I was not a . . . gayboy. Or something.

> When they came for the fox-hunters
> I did not speak out,
> Because I was not a toffee-nosed twat on a horse,
>   with a little trumpet.

> When they came for the smokers
> I did not speak out –
> Because I was not a yellow-fingered ashtray weasel.

> But then they came for me.
> And there was no one left to speak out.

And with this, **Stuart** *passes his empty cereal bowl to the* **Right-Wing
Politician** *and makes his way to the bed.*

*A stunned pause and then, one by one, the panellists begin to clap, and the
audience begins to clap, and then the panellists stand, and so does the
audience. The response is tumultuous.*

Right-Wing Politician   Who was that man?

Pundit   I don't know, but he's turned my head around, I'll
tell you that!

Independent Politician   He's turned everyone's head
around!

The **Presenter** *attempts to get the audience to calm down.*

Presenter   All right, thank you, ladies and gentlemen, can we – ?

But now there is a thumping of chairs.

No please – please put down the furniture –

At this point, someone from the audience rushes up to the stage and throws a chair at the **Presenter***.*

Audience Member   Fascist bastards!

The chair just misses her. He runs out of the doors.

Presenter   Ladies and gentlemen, please stay calm! Please, no smoking, please – please don't light those – don't light that cigarette!

Smoke begins to curl onto the stage. The panellists begin to cough and splutter.

(To panellists.) I think we should go. *(To the audience.)* Ladies and gentlemen – listeners at home – I'm afraid we have no choice but to abandon this week's *Any Questions* due to a stunningly lucid intervention from a member of the public!

Left-Wing Politician *(into mobile)*   Get me the Prime Minister. *(Pause.)* I don't care about that – get him on the phone right now!

Pundit   Keep to the floor where there's air!

They drop to the floor and start to crawl away, a riot occurring in the audience.

Presenter   Next week we'll be in Stevenage – so if you want tickets for that visit our website or call us on 0800-777-444 –

A fireman enters (the actor playing **Mullet***), his torchlight casting a beam through the smoke.*

Mullet   We've got to go now!

He lifts the **Presenter** *over his shoulder and carries her out.*

Presenter   And don't forget *Any Answers* after the break –

She is taken away.

Through the smoke, **Stuart** *is illuminated, sitting cross-legged on the end of his bed. His pot belly makes him look like Buddha.*

The sounds of the audience riot fade.

As the smoke clears, he stands and walks to the front of the stage.

He peers out at the audience, as if looking in a mirror.

Stuart *says only a few of the following statements out loud. The rest are played on tape, creating a collage of sound. During this,* **Angie** *crosses the stage at the back in her dressing gown, towelling her hair; and the* **Right-Wing Politician** *takes her clothes off – she is wearing a nightdress underneath, and now becomes* **Laura**.

Stuart   It's me.
It's Stuart.
It's me again.
I know you're ignoring me.
I know you don't want to speak to me.
I need to speak to you.
I've got some things of yours.
You've got some things of mine.
You should come and get them.
I should come and collect them.
Please call me.
Will you call me?
As soon as you get this.
When you've got the time.
Today if possible.
I'll be in.
Or try my mobile.
But we need to talk.
I'd like to talk.
It'd be good to talk.
I miss you.
I love you.
I made a mistake.

It won't take long.
It's really urgent.
Please.
Please call me.

The smoke clears to reveal **Laura**, *sitting on the toilet.*

Four

[**Stuart** *lies in bed thinking. He tries to masturbate. He hears an ice-cream van outside and contemplates buying one; instead he opens some mail. It is a bill for the council tax. He makes up a little song. He takes a shit. He takes a shower.*]

Stuart   What are you doing?

Laura   What does it look like I'm doing?

Stuart   Number twos?

Laura   No.

Stuart   Number threes?

Laura   What's number threes?

Stuart   Both.

Laura   No, just number ones.

Pause.

Get out then.

Stuart   Why?

Laura   What do you mean, why? Cos I can't pee with you . . . standing there.

Stuart   Why not?

Laura   Cos I just can't. I can't pee with anyone in the room.

Stuart   Try.

Laura   No!

Stuart (*mimics*)   'No!'

Laura   Stuart . . .

Stuart   Do you not love me?

Laura   Yes. What's that got to do with it?

Stuart   'What's love got to do, got to do with it?'

Laura   'What's love but a second-hand emotion?'

Stuart   Do you not trust me?

Laura   Yes. Sort of.

Stuart   Sort of?

Laura   Look, it doesn't matter if I trust you or not, I still can't do the toilet with you sitting there! I can't even do it with my sister in the room.

Stuart   There's lots of stuff you do with me that you wouldn't do with your sister. Well – outside of my masturbatory fantasies.

Laura   You're disgusting. Do you really think about that?

Stuart   What?

Laura   About me doing things with my sister?

Stuart *shrugs.*

Laura   What sort of things?

Stuart   Just being tender and sisterly with each other. Sometimes using a double-ended dildo.

Laura   That's disgusting. You're a dirty old perv.

Pause. He's not leaving.

Please – I'm really desperate.

Stuart   Can't be that desperate.

Pause.

Two people that love each other – they should be able to pee in the same room.

Laura See that's where we differ. I don't think peeing has anything to do with love.

Stuart I don't want you to piss on my face. I just want you to pee with me here in the room.

Laura But why, though?

Stuart I don't know. Because it's something you've never done with anyone else.

Pause.

Laura I don't think I can.

Stuart Try.

Pause. He makes a peeing sound.

Laura I don't think I can.

Stuart Are you worried you'll fart?

Laura No!

Stuart It's all right. Sometimes you need to kick-start the bike. I understand.

Laura I'm not worried I'm going to fart!

Pause.

Stuart Just think of cool, clear water. Flowing. A rushing brook. Niagara Falls. Waves crashing against the pier.

She tries. Pause. A trickle.

Oh – something's happening . . .

Pause. He puts his hand between her legs.

Laura No, it'll stop.

Stuart I just want to feel it.

Pause.

I love everything that comes out of you.

He starts to touch her. She hugs him.

Enter **Angie**.

Angie   What's going on here then?

Music. Bad porn music.

They stop, startled. **Laura** *is still aroused.*

Angie   You don't have a fucking clue what you're doing. Get out of the way.

She pushes **Stuart** *aside and thrusts her hand between* **Laura***'s legs.*

Angie   I'll show you how the little bitch likes it.

Laura *starts to breathe heavily. She clings on to* **Angie**.

Angie   That's it, you little slut. You like that?

Someone in the bed starts to masturbate.

This is how to do it.

Laura   Oh yes, oh yes, that's it – oh finger me, finger me.

Angie (*to* **Stuart**)   Do something useful with yourself and spank my fucking arse.

Stuart *starts to spank* **Angie***'s arse.*

Angie   That's it – spank my big fucking arse!

Mother *appears.*

Mother   Does this dress look terrible on me?

Laura   Oh God, that's so good – oh finger me!

Mother   I've got a bum like a baby elephant.

Stuart (*to* **Mother**)   Go away!

Angie   Spank my big fucking arse!

Mother   It wobbles like a big bloody jelly.

Stuart (*and the bed-wanker simultaneously*)   Go away!

Laura   Oh that's it, that's it, just there –

Angie   Spank me harder, you fucking bastard!

Mother   What do you want for your Christmas?

Laura   Oh God, that's good – rub my little cunt!

Mother   I've got a bum like a baby elephant's.

Mother *slaps her bottom. The rhythm falls into time with* **Stuart***'s spanking of* **Angie***.*

Angie   Spank my big elephant bum!

Laura   What do you want for your Christmas?

Mother   What do you want for your Christmas?

Angie   What do you want for your Christmas, then?

Furious, **Stuart** *gives up. Simultaneously, the girls go limp like dolls and* **Stuart***'s 'double' swings up, out of the bed, to sit on its edge.*

Stuart (*to* **Mother**)   Will you stop going on about your arse?! I don't want to think about your arse! It makes me want to vomit! I don't go on to you about my fucking balls, do I?! How would you like that?!

Pause. He sits on the end of the bed, mirrored in posture by his double.

Pause.

I'm sorry.

Mother   It's all right.

Pause.

Stuart   You know that aftershave stuff you bought me?

Mother   The stuff you said was cheap shite?

Stuart   I know, I know, but listen: I've still got it. And you know, if there was a fire, I wouldn't save my CDs first or my iPod or anything; the first thing I'd save would be that aftershave.

Mother   Don't be silly. If there's a fire you just get on with saving yourself.

Stuart   Well, obviously, yes, but – I'm trying to tell you something. I'm trying to tell you what it means to me.

Pause.

It's funny that, isn't it? Of all the really nice things you gave me – it's the cheap shite that means the most.

Pause.

Will *you* tell her to call me?

Pause. The sound of an ice-cream van. **Laura** *leaves.* **Angie** *bends over the toilet and vomits.* **Stuart** *kneels beside her, rubbing her back.* **Mullet** *bursts in.*

Mullet   Ice cream, ice cream, we all scream for ice scream!

Stuart   Too old for ice cream.

Mullet   What then?

Stuart   Don't know. Sorbet?

Mullet   Fucking sorbet! You're such an old wank! I'll bet you're even starting to like ready-salted!

Stuart   I am, actually.

Mullet   Come on – let's get some ice cream! A 99. Or a push-up.

Stuart   They probably don't have any ice cream. It's probably just smack.

Mullet   Get some of that then.

Stuart   I'll become an addict.

Mullet   So?

Stuart   So then we'll have to live in rubble. You wouldn't like that, would you?

Mullet   You're so boring and fat and emotionally stunted! Go and see if the post's here.

Stuart *looks at his watch.*

Stuart   Fucking should be.

Mullet   Go on then!

Stuart   It'll just be bills.

Mullet   It might not be. It might be a birthday card.

Stuart   It's not my birthday.

Mullet   So?

Pause. They exit, in a kind of synchronicity.

A light breeze blows sand across the stage. The light bulbs sway.

Stuart *enters, opening a bill.*

He stops, and reads it.

Stuart   What the fuck . . . ?

Pause.

I fucking paid that!

He throws it in the bin and puts the kettle on again. Pause.

What a bunch of cunts.

As he waits for the kettle to boil, he repeats the phrase, singing it to himself.

What a bunch of cunts, what a bunch of cunts . . .
What a bunch of cunts, what a bunch of cunts . . .

Music begins. He sings along, the orchestration becoming more elaborate.

Behind him, female dancers appear.

He becomes involved in a song-and-dance number. The lyrics consist only of the words 'What a bunch of cunts' and sometimes 'What a bunch of fucking cunts' for variety's sake.

Male dancers join in – they are blacked-up, like Al Jolson.

[*Note: those of us who grew up in Britain in the seventies were treated, on Saturday nights, to a spectacularly incorrect show called* The Black and White Minstrel Show, *which featured white singers blacked up. The point of this and the following small section might be lost in more enlightened times and locations, and can easily be substituted or omitted. But it should not be omitted on the grounds of offensiveness alone.*]

The song reaches a finale, then ends. Only then does **Stuart** *see the blacked-up male dancers.*

Stuart   What the fuck is this?

Minstrel 1   What?

Stuart   The blacking-up?

Minstrel 1   What about it?

Stuart   What *about* it?

Minstrel 2   We're the Black and White Minstrels.

Stuart   I know who you are. It's a bit fucking racist, isn't it?

Minstrel 3   It was your idea.

Stuart   It wasn't *my* idea.

Minstrel 1   Whose idea was it then?

Minstrel 2   It wasn't fucking mine, that's for sure – I feel a right twat.

Minstrel 3   Me too.

Stuart   It was whoever thought up *The Black and White Minstrels.*

Minstrel 1   Yeah, but you liked it.

Stuart   I didn't like it – it was just on.

Pause.

Right, well, just – fuck off, the lot of you.

Minstrel 2   Don't fucking worry.

Minstrel 1   It *was* your idea.

They leave. **Stuart** *pulls his trousers down and sits on the toilet.*

Stuart   It was just on.

Pause.

Yes, it was a big surprise to me. I'd always thought that you split up with someone because you'd stopped loving them, or realised you never did. But actually none of my relationships – my serious relationships – have ended that way. I've always loved them. There's been some other issue: a different outlook, a different dream; sometimes just practicalities. Nothing you wouldn't love someone for. Just things you can't live with peacefully. But I've felt the loss of every one of them, like a little death. It gets quite tiring after a while, the accumulation of losses.

He wipes his backside and looks at the toilet paper.

The accumulated losses. The accumulated losses of life.

Pause.

My next record? My next record is that one that's got the bit that goes 'I think I love you' that Angie used to play. If you're listening, Angie, please call. You said you'd fucking call.

[Note: this is a reference to the radio programme Desert Island Discs, *in which famous people choose their favourite records. In the original production, this scene ended with a repetitive sample of that one line 'I think I love you', taken from the song 'Take the Box' by Amy Winehouse, but this can be substituted. The point being that we often fixate on one line from a song. The sample then segued into a musical composition which served as the bridge between acts.]*

Music.

Above **Stuart***, a shower unit comes on and he is sprayed with water as he sits there. He turns his face up to it, letting it clean him.*

Lights fade.

Act Two: Afternoon

[**Stuart** *washes his clothes. He is insulted by a telesales call.*]

Stuart, *now dressed, enters with a basket full of dirty washing.*

Stuart (*singing*)
What a bunch of cunts, what a bunch of cunts . . .

*He opens the door of the washing machine and starts bundling the clothes in; but, from inside the machine, he hears his **Mother**'s voice:*

Mother (*muffled*) Have you checked the pockets?

Stuart What?

Mother (*muffled*) Have you looked in the pockets?

He removes some of the washing.

Stuart What are you saying?

Mother I said, have you checked the pockets of your trousers?

Stuart Yes . . .

Mother Are you sure?

Stuart There's nothing in the pockets.

Mother Because you know what happened to those tickets.

Stuart *sighs.*

Mother Why don't you check? Better safe than sorry.

Stuart (*exasperated*) Right, I'll check the fucking trousers.

Mother There's no need for language.

Stuart (*fondly*) There's no need for language.

He drags out a pair of trousers and checks the pockets. He finds something.

Mother What's that? Is that your bus pass?

Stuart   No.

Mother   So much for checking the pockets. Honestly, I think you'd –

Stuart *bundles the washing back in.*

Mother (*muffled*)   – forget your own head if you didn't –

Stuart   Yes, thank you, Mother.

He shuts the door. He empties powder into the tray, not sure how much to add. He sings a jingle from a washing-powder commercial:

'Washing machines live longer with Calgon.'

He crouches down to look at the settings.

What the fuck is a pre-wash? I never do a pre-wash. Maybe I should do a pre-wash?

Pause. He opens the door of the washing machine.

Mum – should I do a pre-wash?

A long pause. There is no answer. Of course not. He closes the door and turns the machine on. It trickles into life.

He looks in the basket. There's a sock in there.

Shit!

He tries to open the door but it's too late.

Exasperated, he takes the sock . . .

Right – you're going in the fucking bin!

. . . and throws it in the pedal bin.

He returns to the machine, watches it turn. The sound of the clothes sloshing.

Bored, he puts the basket on his head and clutches the slats as if they're the bars of a prison cell.

You've got to get me out of here!

This amuses him for a moment.

The sound of the machine gets louder and louder and more hypnotic. It reaches a crescendo and then stops.

The phone rings.

Stuart Hello?!

Salesman Is that Mr McWary?

Stuart Mr McQuarrie.

Salesman Oh, I beg your pardon – Mr McQuarrie: and can I just confirm with you that this is your home number?

Stuart Yes, obviously.

Salesman And is this a BT line, Mr McQuarrie?

Stuart Yes.

Salesman And if I was to tell you that you I could save you up to a hundred pounds a year on your phone bill, would that be of interest to you?

Stuart Em – not really, no.

Salesman I see. And what if I was to tell you that you could also enjoy over twenty extra channels of television at no extra cost – would that be of interest to you?

Stuart No, it wouldn't, but thanks – (for asking).

Salesman And you would also be able to enjoy free broadband at speeds of up to 8 MB depending on your area.

Stuart I'm sorry, but I'm really not interested. And I'm actually not that keen on being – (phoned at home).

Salesman Because all that can be yours with Teleport's Essentials package at an introductory price of just £13.99 a month for the first three months.

Stuart Right, well, you don't seem to be listening to me, but I'm really not interested, I'm sorry.

Pause.

Salesman You're not interested?

Stuart   Sorry, no.

A pause, and then the **Salesman** *hangs up.*

Stuart   Hello?

Nothing.

Fucking cheeky bastard!

Mullet *appears from under the bedding.*

Mullet   You are one totally pathetic fucking loser!

Stuart   What?

Mullet   That guy just made an absolute cunt of you.

Stuart   I know he did!

Mullet   He made a fucking tit of you in your own house.

Stuart   I know!

Mullet   And you just let it happen.

Stuart   Well, what was I supposed to do? I said I wasn't interested – I was trying to be polite.

Mullet   Exactly. He basically said, 'I'm going to fuck you up the arse,' and you said, 'Yes, sir,' and spread your fat arse-cheeks.

Stuart   Cheeky fucking bastard!

Mullet   So what are you going to do about it?

The phone rings.

Stuart   Hello?

Salesman   Hello, is that Mr McWary?

Mullet *urges him on.*

Stuart   If by Mr McWary you mean Mr McQuarrie, then yes.

Mullet *is disgusted with him.*

Salesman   Oh, I beg your pardon – Mr McQuarrie: and can I just confirm with you that this is your – (home number)?

Mullet   Is that it?

Stuart   Eh?

Mullet   'If by Mr McWary you mean Mr McQuarrie' – is that all you're worried about? That he got your name wrong?

Stuart   I was just starting.

Mullet   You still said yes though, didn't you?

Stuart   What am I supposed to say?

Mullet   Tell the cunt to fuck off!

The phone rings.

Stuart   Hello?

Salesman   Hello, is that Mr McWary?

Stuart   No, it fucking isn't!

Stuart *looks at* **Mullet**.

Salesman   Oh – I'm sorry –

Mullet   Tell him to fuck off!

Stuart   Fuck off!

Pause. They seem pleased with themselves.

Salesman   Hello?

Stuart   He's still there!

Mullet   Give it to the cunt!

Stuart   Give him what?

Mullet   It's a Saturday afternoon, for fuck's sake!

Stuart   It's a Saturday afternoon, for fuck's sake!

Mullet *nods.*

Stuart   Would you like me phoning you on a Saturday afternoon?

Pause.

No, I didn't think so; and I don't want any more shit TV channels so fuck off and don't call me again!

The phone hangs up.

That told him.

Mullet   Yeah, but he still hung up on *you*. He's still got the power. He's phoned you up at your house, on your day off, and he's made you feel angry and bad.

Stuart   What can I do about it?

Mullet   Make *him* regret calling *you*. Spoil *his* fucking day!

Pause.

Stuart   All right.

The phone rings.

Hello?

Salesman   Hello, is that Mr McWary?

Stuart   No, it's Mr McQuarrie.

Mullet *is annoyed with him. but* **Stuart** *indicates to wait.*

Salesman   Oh, I beg your pardon – Mr McQuarrie. And could you just confirm that this is your home number?

Stuart   Yes it is. But listen – are you calling from Teleport?

Pause.

Salesman   Yes, I am.

Stuart   Oh good, I was hoping you'd call.

Pause.

Salesman   Were you?

Stuart Yes, and listen, I'm very interested in your product but would you mind calling back in about ten minutes? It's just that I'm wanking at the moment.

Salesman I'm sorry?

Stuart I said I'm wanking at the moment – but I should have come in about five minutes so if you could call back then, that'd be perfect.

Mullet *is delighted.*

Salesman Oh – right . . .

Stuart I mean, unless you'd like to stay on the line and talk me through it, you know – say something like, 'Ooh yes, ooh yes, wank it,' over and over again. Would that interest you at all, you little fucking maggot?

Pause.

I'm asking you a question, you subhuman piece of shit – would that interest you?

Salesman No, sir – it wouldn't.

Stuart Right – well, then, *you* can fuck off!

The phone goes dead. They are triumphant. They run around whooping in triumph.

Mullet That was fucking great!

Stuart He'll think twice about doing that again.

Mullet God, you were quite vicious there. 'Subhuman piece of shit'?

Stuart Well, I'll take abuse up to a certain point –

Mullet Yeah, but there's a line.

Stuart But there's a line, and if you cross it – doesn't matter who you are –

Mother Stuart!

They both jump out of their skins.

Mother   Stuart McQuarrie! What do you think you're playing at?!

Stuart   What?

Mother   Don't 'what' me! I heard the filth you were saying! What was the meaning of it?

Stuart   I didn't start it.

Mother   Who did then?

Stuart   The guy on the phone – he called me up, out of the blue –

Mother   I know what he did. I don't remember him saying any filth to you.

Stuart   No, well, he didn't; but when I said I wasn't interested, he just hung up on me. Which was pretty bloody rude.

She slaps him round the head.

Mother   There's no need for language!

Stuart   You shouldn't hit people on the head, it gives them brain damage.

Mother   I'll brain damage you.

Pause.

So he hung up on you. Which was rude . . .

Stuart   So I decided to be rude back.

Mother   Oh, the Big Man, is it? The Head Cheese.

Mullet *smirks.*

Mother   Making someone feel small over the phone.

Stuart   He hung up on me.

Mother   Did he? Are you sure that's what happened? Let's ask him, shall we?

Stuart   Ask him?

Mother   Yes – because he's here. Simon?!

She looks offstage.

Come and give him a hand.

Stuart *and* **Mullet** *look at* **Simon** *– who we cannot yet see – and then at each other.*

Mother   Come on then.

She nods them in an offstage direction. **Stuart** *makes* **Mullet** *acompany him. They exit.*

Muffled sounds of effort offstage.

They return with **Simon***. He's in a wheelchair, attached to an IV drip.* **Mother** *helps bring him onstage. One of* **Simon***'s arms is tiny and malformed.*

Mother   Simon, this – I'm ashamed to say – is my son. Stuart – this is the man you called subhuman.

Simon   Hello.

He extends his small hand. **Stuart** *and* **Mullet** *shake it.*

Stuart   Hello.

Mullet   Hi.

Simultaneously:

Simon   Why don't you –

Mother   Listen, I just –

Simon   Sorry –

Mother   No, you go ahead.

Simon   I just wanted to say that it's really all right. I completely understand – we get enough adverts thrown at us without people calling you up at home and trying to sell things. Believe me, I feel embarrassed every time I call someone. It's just that, obviously, given my condition, you know – playing for England was never an option.

Stuart   Oh, I don't know . . .

Mother   Stuart!

Stuart   Oh well, look – I'm sorry that you're disabled and all that and obviously I feel a bit bad. But it doesn't change the fact that as soon as I said I wasn't interested, you just hung up on me; and that's just rude, whatever . . . condition you're in.

Mother   Oh, and you're such a big know-it-all, aren't you? The Big I-Am. Well, tell him, Simon.

Simon   Oh really, it's all right. He wasn't to know.

Pause.

Stuart   Wasn't to know what?

Mother   It just so happens, Mr Smarty-Pants, that Simon didn't hang up on you; he actually had a seizure.

Pause.

Simon   I felt it coming on during the conversation. I'd have said goodbye but my jaw sort of locks, so I can't speak.

Pause.

Mother   Thank you, Simon.

Pause.

I hope you're proud of yourself, Stuart McQuarrie. Maybe you'll not be so quick to judge in future.

She wheels him offstage.

Stuart *and* **Mullet** *are left there, in their shame.*

The sound of the washing machine turning.

Mullet *sits by it and puts the basket on his head, as* **Stuart** *had earlier.*

Stuart *makes his way back to the couch.*

Pause.

The **Cat** *ambles slowly in.*

Stuart   Ah, here he is. Where have you been all night? Chasing all the girl cats I bet.

Cat   Fuck you.

*The **Cat** walks straight to the bowl of cat food and smells it.*

Cat   Muck.

And with this, he turns and walks slowly out again.

Stuart *tries to stroke him as he passes, but the **Cat** shrugs him off.*

Angie *enters. She's trying on clothes for an evening out.*

Angie   What's wrong with Galloway?

Stuart   He's spoiled.

Angie   Well, if he's spoiled it's because you spoiled him.

Stuart   I don't spoil him. They must have been feeding him salmon or something.

Angie   At a rescue centre? I doubt it. Anyway, don't change the subject.

Stuart   What was the subject?

Angie   You being a homophobe.

Pause.

Pleading the Fifth, I see.

Stuart   I don't care if you think I'm a homophobe. I know I'm not.

Angie   But being gay revolts you?

Stuart   I didn't say being *gay* revolts me.

Angie   What did you say then?

Stuart   I don't care if people are gay. I'm actually in favour of it.

Angie   Why, because it narrows the competition?

Stuart   Exactly. And they're all the best-looking guys as well. Everybody wins.

Angie   You said it revolts you.

Stuart   No, I said that if you're a heterosexual man –
regardless of how enlightened you are – you find the thought
of, you know –

Angie   What?

Stuart   The thought of coming into direct contact with
another man's . . .

Angie   Cock.

Stuart   Yes –

Angie   You can't even say it.

Stuart   Can't even say what?

Angie   Another man's cock.

Stuart   Another man's cock.

Angie   There, you see? Still heterosexual.

She kisses him.

Stuart   You are so fucking annoying, d'you know that?

Angie   And you're a homophobe.

Pause.

And a racist.

Stuart   How am I a fucking racist now?!

Angie   Cos every time you tell me what Mr Rajah's said you
put on that stupid accent.

Stuart   That's not being racist.

Angie   It is so . . . 'All reduced – Mr Rajah's all reduced!'

Stuart   That's how he talks!

Angie   You don't have to do the wee shake of the head.

Stuart   So *The Simpsons* is racist, is it?

Angie   Yes.

Pause.

Stuart   I'm not a fucking racist. There's not a racist bone in my body. In fact I go out of my way to not be racist.

Angie   How?

Stuart   Well – if an Asian shopkeeper –

Angie   'An Asian shopkeeper – '

Stuart   Yes – if an Asian shopkeeper gives me change, I always make a point of just making slight contact with his hand.

Angie   What's that supposed to prove?

Stuart   Well, you know – just to make sure he knows I don't think I'll get the Paki touch or something. And – if I get on a bus, and there's an Asian person sitting there –

Angie   Don't tell me – you sit beside them.

Stuart   Yes! Even if there are other seats!

Angie   You are such a fucking wanker, Stuart McQuarrie.

Stuart   Ah, but who's more of a wanker? The wanker, or the wanker that loves the wanker?

She pushes him away.

Angie   I don't love you.

Pause.

You love me.

Stuart   Yes. I do.

He embraces her. Pause.

Angie   D'you want to shag?

Pause. He looks at his watch.

Stuart   Yeah, all right.

She pulls him down behind the couch. We hear their voices, as they struggle off with their clothes.

Stuart   Can you bum your girlfriend?

Angie   Can I bum my girlfriend?

Stuart   Can *one* bum one's girlfriend? I mean – you hear about men bumming each other but you never hear someone say, 'I bummed my girlfriend.'

Angie   I'll fucking bum you.

Stuart   You'll bum me?

Angie   Will you shut the fuck up?!

We hear the sound of them starting to make love.

Father *enters and stops as he sees them.*

Father   What's going on here?!

Suddenly, from behind the couch, up spring **Stuart** *and* **Laura***, looking flustered.*

Mullet *suddenly springs into life.*

Mullet   Stewpot, look! Porno!

He waves a tatty old porno mag that he's found.

Stuart   Not now!

Laura *runs out, distressed, clutching her blouse to her chest.*

Stuart *half follows her.*

Stuart   Laura!

Mullet *finds more pornography in the sand.*

Mullet   There's more, look! It's like treasure!

Angie *appears from behind the couch.*

Angie   You dirty bastard!

She storms out.

Stuart   Angie – it's not mine!

Mullet   Look at this!

Stuart *runs to* **Mullet**.

Stuart   I can't just now.

Mullet   But look at the fanny on that!

Stuart   Christ.

Mother (*enters*)   Stuart!

Stuart   I've got to go

Mullet   Later, then.

Stuart   Yeah, later.

Mother   Stuart, get over here now!

He runs back and sits on the couch, shamefaced.

Father   Well, I think we have to tell them.

Mother   Oh, shut your silly mouth. We don't have to tell anyone anything.

Father   If it was the other way round, we'd want to know.

Mother   Have you met Laura's parents?

Father   No, but – (that's not the point).

Mother   Then shut your silly mouth, you old jessie.

Father   Don't call me a jessie, Margaret. Not in front of Stuart.

Mother (*mimics*)   'Don't call me a jessie, don't call me a jessie.'

Father   Right, well, you sort it out then; because I give up, I just bloody give up!

He walks out.

Mother   'I just bloody give up.'

Stuart *and his* **Mother** *share a conspiratorial laugh.*

Pause.

Mother   So – what are we going to do with the two of you?

Pause. **Stuart** *shrugs.*

Mother   He may be an old jessie, but you know what they say, even a stopped clock's right twice a day. When we've got Laura under our roof, we've got a duty of care. We've got a responsibility, to make sure she doesn't get up to anything that her parents wouldn't want her getting up to. You know what Jesus said: 'Suffer the little children.'

Stuart *looks confused.*

Mother   What do you think of her?

She pokes at him.

Stuart. Stuart.

Stuart   Who?!

Mother   Don't act the daft laddie. What do you think of Laura?

Pause.

Do you love her?

Pause. He shrugs uncomfortably.

Just a shrug.

Stuart   Aw, Mum!

Mother   Don't 'Aw, Mum' me, it's important. You put your swizzle-stick inside a girl and babies are what's next.

Stuart *groans and puts a cushion over his head.*

Mother   Now don't be such a baby. It's a thing for a girl that age to have a child. She's just a little thing too. She's not got a big fat bum and hips like me. A baby'd rip her from front to back.

Stuart *groans. She prises the cushion away from him.*

Mother   Listen to me, Stuart. You know what Jesus said: 'Respect your mother.'

Stuart   He never said that!

Mother   You weren't there, you don't know. Now listen to me: do you get all excited when you think of her? And I don't mean your swizzle-stick –

Stuart   Stop saying that!

Mother   I mean, down your back, a little shiver. And do you want to say her name over and over? Do you find excuses to say it? Laura Laura Laura!

She teases him.

And do you hug the pillow and pretend it's her?

He throws the cushion aside.

Stuart   No!

Mother   Ah, you see – a picture tells a hundred tales.

Pause.

And is it like all the other girls just disappear? Like they don't exist? Like she's the only girl in the world?

(Sings.)
    'If you were the only girl in the world,
    And I was the only boy . . . '

She smiles. Pause.

Well, you listen to me –

He covers his ears. She wrenches the cushion away, so seriously it startles him.

I'm being serious, Stuart, this is important!

Pause.

Don't you pay any mind to what anyone says. There's nothing worse you can do in this world than marry for the sake of appearance. If you feel all those things about a girl, then maybe she's the one. But if you don't, or if you think you might not feel them ten years down the line, then you let her go, no matter how she cries; and do it sooner, not later. Let her be free to find someone who does feel that. You be alone rather than that; rather than fight like cat and dog all your life; rather than die a bit at a time. That's what a real man does for a woman. That's what he does for himself.

Pause.

Don't you settle for less than love, than true love, do you hear me? Don't you settle for less!

Pause.

Laura *enters.*

Mother   Here she is.

Laura *sits on the couch with* **Stuart**.

Mother   You feeling better?

Laura *nods.*

Laura   I like your mirror.

Mother   Which?

Laura   The big one in the hall.

Mother   That was my mother's. Yes.

Pause.

My mother gave that to me.

Classical music plays, and **Stuart** *lies down to listen to it. With one hand, he half conducts.*

Mother, *bare-footed and parasol in hand, walks across the sand.*

[*Note: in the original production, this next scene played out as if on a beach, but the location, in itself, is unimportant and you may wish to change it depending on your stage design.*]

Mother *walks around a rock pool. She stares up at the sun.*

Suddenly she becomes unsteady on her feet, totters slightly, and then collapses, face down.

Bystander 1, *who has been talking on his mobile phone, runs to her. He crouches down beside her, unsure what to do.*

Bystander 2 *rushes in, having seen the collapse.*

Bystander 1 *calls for an ambulance.*

Seeing a coastguard, **Bystander 2** *rushes offstage towards him.*

Father *enters, in holiday clothes, carrying a bag of shopping. When he sees his wife collapsed, he drops his shopping and runs to her, but it is too late.*

He cradles her in his arms.

Bystander 2 *returns. Lights fade on this tableau. The music ends. The washing machine churns to a halt.*

Act Three: Night

[**Stuart** *has something to eat. He watches television. He goes to bed.*]

Stuart *looks at his watch.*

He gets up and goes to the fridge, opens it.

He takes out a ready meal.

Laura *enters.*

Laura   Oh Stuart!

Stuart   What?

Laura   What's that?

Stuart   It's a prawn curry thing.

Laura *is disapproving*

Laura   What?

Laura   I'll bet it's full of E-numbers.

Stuart   What's wrong with E-numbers?

Laura   They're bad for you.

Stuart   Everything's bad for you.

He pierces the film, puts the meal in the microwave and starts it cooking.

Laura   You shouldn't use microwaves either. They make you infertile.

Stuart   Good. Won't have to bother with johnnies.

Laura   Don't say good. What if we want to have children?

Stuart   Laura, for fuck's sake – will you get off my back? If you want to go out with a leaf-eating, non-smoking, rice-eating wank then do it. But stop trying to turn me into one.

Pause.

Laura   I'm just saying it because I don't want you to die.

Stuart   Awww.

Laura   Who'll look after all the animals if you die?

Stuart   Oh I don't *know* . . .

Laura   Oh, oh – I've thought of another one! Koala bears! We've got to have some koala bears!

Stuart   Aren't they vicious?

Laura   Koala bears? They're lovely!

Stuart   I stand corrected.

Laura   But we'll have to grow eucalyptus trees because that's all they eat.

Stuart   Yeah, well – we're growing bamboo for the pandas anyway.

Laura   I think we'll have to build another biosphere, just for plants.

Stuart   This started out as a small farmhouse in France and now it's like Blofeld's fucking secret complex. Who's going to pay for all this?

Laura   I am!

Stuart   You are? Because it's going to cost about a billion pounds.

Laura   Yeah, well, it's a dream house. You can't put a price on a dream house!

She exits.

Stuart   You can't put a price on a dream house . . .

The microwave pings.

Stuart *takes out the meal. He peels back the film, stirs it, then places it back inside.*

He sits on the couch. The light from the TV on his face.

Stuart   *The Golden Shot, The Generation Game . . . Bullseye, Deal or No Deal.* [*Substitute if necessary, both here and later.*]

For a moment, **Stuart** *is only lit by the TV. His face fixes into an inane grin. A high-pitched noise sounds.*

The doorbell rings. Lights up again. **Stuart** *looks puzzled.*

The doorbell rings again. He gets up to answer it, leaving the stage.

The light bulbs sway. A breeze shifts the sand. Pause.

Paul *enters, carrying a bag.* **Stuart** *is displeased.*

Paul   I know, I know – you said you were doing nothing.

Stuart   Yeah, and I sort of meant it.

Paul   Yeah, well, there was nothing going on at the Duck. Fucking girlfriends, I'm telling you – they're ruining the world. D'you want to stick these in the fridge?

He hands him some cans of beer. **Stuart** *groans.*

Paul   We don't have to drink them all. We'll just have a beer and see how it goes; if you still 'vant to be alone', I'll piss off – Scout's honour.

Stuart *puts them in the fridge.*

Paul *sits on the couch. He unwraps some food.*

Paul   I got you some chips.

Stuart   I just put something in the microwave.

Paul   What?

Stuart   A prawn curry.

Paul   That'll go with chips. What's this? *Millionaire?*

He opens a can of beer and hands one to **Stuart***, then opens one for himself. They fill their glasses.*

Paul   Look at this cunt. He's used a lifeline already and he's not even up to five hundred.

Stuart*, resigned to his fate, sits on the couch beside him.*

Paul   D – Jon Pertwee.

Again only the TV light plays on their faces. They stare at the television, with those same inane grins. The same whining sound. It suddenly ends and they return to normality.

Paul   That was shite. It's about time they put that to bed. What's on the other side?

Stuart   Let's just see the headlines.

Again – the light, the grins, the sound. Lights up.

Paul   The Israelis are a deeply misunderstood people.

Stuart   Fuck . . .

Paul   What?

Stuart   I had a dream . . . something to do with Israel . . .

Paul   What's this?

Once more – the lights, the sound. but only **Stuart** *is grinning.* **Paul** *immediately falls asleep. Lights up.* **Paul** *wakes.*

Paul   Who did it?

Stuart   The guy with the haircut.

Paul   His mate?

Stuart   Yeah.

Paul   Told you. Shall we partake of another 'tinnie'?

Stuart   Yeah, go on.

Paul   On you go then.

Stuart   Me?

Paul   You're the host.

Stuart   Didn't get much choice in the matter, did I?

Pause. He sighs.

These are nice chips.

He gets up to go to the fridge. **Paul** *watches him intently.*

Stuart   Fuck . . .

Pause.

Paul   What is it?

Pause.

Stuart   I feel really funny.

Pause.

Fuck . . .

He drops to his knees. The chips spill out of his hand across the floor.

Paul, I'm not joking – something's really wrong . . .

He rolls on to his back. **Paul** *gets up to look at him.*

Stuart   Call – an ambulance –

Paul   Can you move?

Stuart   No –

Paul   Try and move your hand.

Pause. Nothing.

Stuart   Oh Jesus – what's happening to me?

Pause. **Paul** *looks around. He takes a cushion from the couch.*

He squats down beside **Stuart**.

Stuart   Paul –

Paul   Have you got anything to say?

Stuart *can barely even make a sound.*

Paul   Stuart – look at me; have you got anything to say –
you *cunt.*

Pause. With great effort:

Stuart   Tell Angie – that I love her. Tell her – I don't know –
why I left her – like I did.

Pause. **Paul** *nods.*

He places the cushion over **Stuart***'s face.*

We hear his muffled shouts for a while, then they fade.

After a while, **Paul** *removes the cushion.*

Breathing heavily, **Paul** *stares down at* **Stuart***'s corpse.*

The doorbell rings, startling him.

For a moment he doesn't know what to do.

The doorbell rings again.

Paul   There in a minute!

With great effort, he drags **Stuart***'s body out of sight.*

Mullet *appears, peering over the back of the couch, watching this.*

The doorbell rings again.

Paul *enters, out of breath.*

Paul   Just a moment!

And then he sees **Mullet***. Their eyes meet.* **Paul** *puts his finger to his mouth – 'Shhhhh.'*

Paul *straightens himself up and goes to answer the door.*

The light bulbs sway.

Voices offstage.

Paul   Angie, hi.

Angie   Hi, Paul. Is Stuart here?

They enter.

Paul   Eh – he's not, actually.

Angie   Where is he?

Paul   I don't know. Is he not with you?

Angie   No, why? Did he say he was seeing me?

Paul   I think so . . .

Angie   No. I was meant to give him a call but I wasn't seeing him. Not as far as I know.

Paul   Oh right. I thought that was what he said.

She looks around the flat. **Paul**, *nervous, positions himself in front of where he dragged* **Stuart**'s *body.*

Angie   What are you doing here?

Paul   Do you want a beer or something?

Angie   No, I'm all right.

Pause.

What are you doing here?

Paul   We were down the Duck's Arse, you know – earlier. Had a couple of pints and then we were coming back here, but he had to do something – I thought he said he was seeing you, or calling you or something. So he said for me to wait here. I thought that was him.

She nods, obviously suspicious.

Angie   When was this?

Paul   Eight or so. I mean, I tried phoning him but . . .

Their talk fades, to be replaced by music. This is what we would hear them saying (or as much as you need for the moment).

Paul   . . . it always seems to be busy. I don't know, I just assumed maybe he was on the phone to you. To be honest I assumed you were maybe having a bit of a barney. Sorry, but you know how it is. Best not to interfere with these things. So, you know – I just made myself comfortable here, had a few beers, watched the TV, that sort of thing. But I am getting a wee bit worried. It's been a couple of hours now and if he wasn't seeing you, then I don't know who he could have been seeing. It isn't really like him whichever way you look at it.

Angie   No it's not.

Paul I don't know – what do you think we should do? Maybe we should go out looking for him. I'm sure there's some explanation for it. Maybe he met someone. We could always try the Duck, maybe he's gone back there. I did sort of foist myself on him. Maybe he had some other plans that he didn't want to tell me about.

But instead . . .

A spotlight – signifying **Angie***'s point of view – moves across the floor, highlighting: the two glasses of beer, the two cans, the spilled chips and then the tracks left in the sand by* **Stuart***'s dragged body. The spotlight follows the tracks off into the wings.*

Mullet *still watches, silently, from behind the couch.*

The sound returns.

Paul No, I'm sure there's an explanation for it.

Pause.

Angie (*scared*) I'll try phoning him.

Paul I've tried him a few times. There's no answer.

Pause.

Angie Can't hurt to try again.

Pause.

Paul Tell you what – let's try down the Duck. We can give him a call on the way.

He puts his jacket on. Pause.

Angie All right.

They exit. **Angie** *casts a look backwards as she leaves.*

Pause. The sand shifts again.

A mobile phone starts ringing: it's the sound of an ice-cream van.

Mullet *slowly appears from behind the couch. He sits down cross-legged and starts eating the chips from the floor.*

Music.

From everywhere come the mourners, all moving slowly.

Laura *looks like a grieving supermodel, her movements strangely jerky as she walks to position.*

Stuart's **Father** *enters slowly, in a black suit.*

Stuart's **Mother**, *all in white, descends from the ceiling to come to a stop only feet above the ground.*

The **Cat**, *Galloway, enters, dragging a dead bird.*

They take their positions around the room, forming a bizarre tableau.

The music ends.

Mother   I remember one winter, it had just snowed – this was back when it snowed in winter – I looked out of the window of our house, down into the square, and I saw him in his little school uniform –

Father   He could never keep his shirt-tails in, could he?

Mother   No, that's right. Or his laces done up. But anyway, I looked down and – before he came into the stair – I saw him deliberately rolling in the snow, you know; getting it all over himself. So I'd make a fuss of him when he came in. Give him a nice bowl of home-made soup. I think that was the only thing I cooked that he actually liked.

Pause.

Laura   Yeah, cos I remember when it was snowing; and I think we'd had a bit of an argument. No, I think we'd actually split up; yeah, that's right. And we both spent about a week in misery but not knowing if the other one was bothered. And then one morning I came out of my mum's house to go to school and all this snow had fallen and it was all untouched; except outside my door, and on all the cars, and everywhere, someone had written 'I love you Laura'. Everywhere you could see.

Mother   Stuart?

Laura   He must've got up really early and come over to my house and done it all before I got up.

Mother   He did love you, Laura. I know you had your ups and downs; but he really did. And you, Angie. But I think you've always got a soft spot for the first.

Angie *shrugs, absorbing the veiled insult.*

Father   Well, that must've been the only time he ever got up early. D'you remember – he got into terrible trouble for being late at school?

Mother   Oh dear, yes. What a palaver that was. They had us in, didn't they?

Father   They were going to expel him!

Mother   That's right, they were.

Father   They were going to expel him if he was late just once more. So he came up with this foolproof system – he put a bucket of cold water by his bed. The theory being, when his alarm clock went off, rather than just turning it off and going back to sleep as usual, he would immediately plunge his whole head into this bucket of water. Well – come the morning – off goes the alarm, Stuart bolts awake, rolls over – takes one look at the water, says, 'Not a chance,' and just goes back to sleep again!

Laughter.

Angie   If he had to leave before me in the morning, he'd always put one of my teddy bears in bed beside me, with its little arm over me.

Affectionate nodding. Pause.

Mother   Galloway – you must have a few stories about Stuart?

Pause. Galloway considers it.

Cat   He was a prick.

Pause. **Father** *raises his glass.*

Father   To Stuart.

They raise their glasses.

All   To Stuart.

Music.

Stuart *appears now. They all turn to see him.*

They begin to clap. They applaud him as he walks down to them, his arms open, almost messianic.

He kisses **Angie**.

He shakes his **Father***'s hand and tries, awkwardly, to hug him.*

He hugs his **Mother** *tight.*

He attempts to stroke Galloway, but the **Cat** *swipes him with his claws.*

He high-fives **Mullet**.

Finally, he embraces **Laura**.

Laura *and* **Angie** *remove his clothes until he is as he was at the beginning of the play.*

His **Father** *and* **Mother** *prepare his bed.*

The **Cat** *picks up the dead bird and leaves.*

Stuart *is led up to the bed. His* **Father** *tucks him under the covers. His* **Mother** *kisses his forehead. They exit.*

Mullet *takes one last look at his friend, peaceful in bed now, then leaves.*

The bed slowly lifts up to a vertical position. Over this:

Stuart (*on tape*)
  And now I lay me down to sleep
  I pray the Lord my soul to keep
  And if I die before I wake
  I pray my soul the Lord to take.

Stuart *sleeps, as if we are looking down on him.*

The phone rings. He wakes and answers it. **Angie** *is voice only.*

Stuart   Hello?

Angie   Stuart? It's Angie. Did I wake you?

Stuart   Eh – no, no.

Angie   Are you in bed?

Stuart   Yeah, but I'm awake. I thought you were going to call me.

Angie   I am calling you.

Stuart   I thought you were going to call me earlier.

Pause.

Angie   You wanted to speak to me.

Stuart   Yes, of course –

Pause.

Angie   I don't care about my things. Throw them away if you want.

Pause.

Stuart   That's not what I wanted to say . . .

Angie   What then?

Stuart   Is it a bad time?

Angie   A bad time?

Stuart   You seem in a hurry.

Angie   It's late.

Stuart   Whose fault is that?

Angie   Don't start or I'll hang up.

Stuart   Don't hang up.

Angie   Then say what you've got to say.

Pause.

Stuart   Jesus, Angie – does it have to be like this?

Angie   Like what?

Stuart   Look – I know you won't believe me, Angie. But I love you. I really do.

Pause.

Angie   Stuart . . .

Stuart   And I know, so why did I finish it? But you've got to believe me when I say – I don't know. I truly don't know. There was no reason for it; I'm not seeing anyone else, I wasn't unhappy. I didn't do it because of what's happening now. I did it because – of what would happen in the future.

Pause.

Angie   Why are you telling me this?

Stuart   Because I don't want to live without you.

Pause.

Angie   What does that mean?

Stuart   It means what it means. It means that I love you. That's a precious thing. Do you know how precious that is?

Pause.

I know you're hurt. But let's not throw everything away.

Angie   You're really confusing me.

Pause.

What are you saying? Are you saying you regret it – what?

Long pause.

Stuart   No. I'm not saying I regret it. I think it was the right thing to do, for both of our sakes. But I didn't do it because I don't love you.

Pause.

Why don't we meet up?

Angie   No.

Stuart   Why not?

Angie   You know why not.

Pause.

It's over, Stuart. It has to be.

Pause.

Stuart   We can't even be friends?

Angie   I don't know. Not now.

Stuart   But some day.

Angie   I don't know. Maybe – who knows? But for now – stop calling me. Please. Please, Stuart.

Pause.

I have to go now.

Stuart   Not like this.

Angie   What do you mean?

Stuart   I mean let's not make it a big goodbye. I can't handle it, not just now.

Pause.

Just talk to me for a while. Talk to me like we'll be seeing each other tomorrow.

Pause.

Angie   What do you want me to say?

Stuart   I don't know. Anything.

Pause.

Angie   How's Galloway?

Stuart   He's fine. Surly, as usual.

Pause.

Angie   What did you do today?

Stuart Today?

Pause.

Fuck all.

The lights by now have faded to black.

Optional Epilogue

[In the original production, the following happened. Obviously, it was an expensive sequence and the play will work without it. If it can be done, it should be, but it may be omitted if there is no reasonable way to achieve it.]

A box is flown in.

When the lights come up, it is revealed as a kitchen. The furniture – the washing machine, the cooker, the fridge, etc – is exactly the same as that which was dotted around the set, but is now in its proper place. It looks very real.

A door opens and **Stuart** *enters. He then proceeds to make himself, in real time and with little fuss, a cup of tea. This done, he sits at the kitchen table.*

Angie *enters, wearing a dressing gown. She takes the washing out of the washing machine (a stray red sock has caused the whites to come out pink). Irritated, she leaves.*

Stuart *sits there.*

The lights come up. The audience gradually realise they are expected to leave. **Stuart** *continues drinking his tea.*

Eventually, the theatre empties.